LANGUAGE AND THE
ENGLISH CURRICULUM

Open University Press

English, Language, and Education series

General Editor: Anthony Adams

Lecturer in Education, University of Cambridge

SELECTED TITLES IN THE SERIES

The Problem with Poetry
Richard Andrews

Writing Development
Roslyn Arnold

Writing Policy in Action
Eve Bearne and Cath Farrow

Secondary Worlds
Michael Benton

Time for Drama
Roma Burgess and Pamela Gaudry

Thinking Through English
Paddy Creber

Developing Response to Poetry
Patrick Dias and Michael Hayhoe

Developing English
Peter Dougill (ed.)

The Primary Language Book
Peter Dougill and Richard Knott

Children Talk About Books
Donald Fry

English at the Core
Peter Griffith

Literary Theory and English Teaching
Peter Griffith

Lesbian and Gay Issues in the English Classroom
Simon Harris

Reading and Response
Mike Hayhoe and Stephen Parker (eds)

Assessing English
Brian Johnston

Lipservice: The Story of Talk in Schools
Pat Jones

Language and the English Curriculum
John Keen

Shakespeare in the Classroom
Susan Leach

Oracy Matters
Margaret MacLure, Terry Phillips and Andrew Wilkinson (eds)

Language Awareness for Teachers
Bill Mittins

Beginning Writing
John Nichols *et al.*

Teaching Literature for Examinations
Robert Protherough

Developing Response to Fiction
Robert Protherough

The Making of English Teachers
Robert Protherough and Judith Atkinson

Young People Reading
Charles Sarland

English Teaching from A–Z
Wayne Sawyer, Anthony Adams and Ken Watson

Reconstructing 'A' Level English
Patrick Scott

School Writing
Yanina Sheeran and Douglas Barnes

Reading Narrative as Literature
Andrew Stibbs

Collaboration and Writing
Morag Styles (ed.)

Reading Within and Beyond the Classroom
Dan Taverner

Reading for Real
Barrie Wade (ed.)

English Teaching in Perspective
Ken Watson

The Quality of Writing
Andrew Wilkinson

The Writing of Writing
Andrew Wilkinson (ed.)

Spoken English Illuminated
Andrew Wilkinson, Alan Davies and Deborah Berrill

LANGUAGE AND THE ENGLISH CURRICULUM

John Keen

Open University Press
Buckingham • Philadelphia

Open University Press
Celtic Court
22 Ballmoor
Buckingham
MK18 1XW

and
1900 Frost Road, Suite 101
Bristol, PA 19007, USA

First Published 1992

A catalogue record of this book is available
from the British Library

Library of Congress Cataloging-in-Publication Data

Keen, John, 1949–
    Language and the English curriculum / John Keen.
       p.   cm. — (English, language, and education)
    Includes bibliographical references (p.) and index.
    ISBN 0–335–09673–5
    1. English language—Study and teaching (Secondary)—Great
Britain.   2. Language arts (Secondary)—Great Britain.   3. Language
experience approach in education—Great Britain.   I. Title.
II. Series: English, language, and education series.
LB1631.K38   1992
428′.0071′241—dc20
                                         91–45502
                                          CIP

Typeset by Graphicraft Typesetters Limited, Hong Kong
Printed in Great Britain by St Edmundsbury Press Limited
Bury St Edmunds, Suffolk

Contents

General editor's introduction

I first came across the work of John Keen through a reading of his earlier book, *Teaching English: A Linguistic Approach* (1978), which was very heavily influenced by the programme directed by Professor M. A. K. Halliday at University College, London, on Linguistics in the English Curriculum. This produced a number of important products, notably the *Breakthrough to Literacy* programme (Mackay *et al*. 1970) and Doughty, Pearce and Thornton's *Language in Use* (1971). It also led to the production of a wide ranging collection of books edited by Doughty and Thornton on areas of what they came to call 'linguistic science'. John Keen's book was a contribution in this field and certainly helped me as a new recruit to the business of teacher education to find ways of enabling my students to understand the importance of the linguistic elements within the English curriculum.

Much has happened since then and, in England and Wales especially, the National Curriculum has ensured that teachers of English have come to see themselves as having a responsibility for language education. Several recent publications in this series have emphasized this and, in particular, W. H. Mittins's *Language Awareness for Teachers* (1991) seeks to give a comprehensive overview of those aspects of linguistic science that teachers, not just of English but other subjects also, need to be acquainted with. At the same time we are seeing the rapid growth of A Level English Language courses and there is no doubt of the motivation of school students to embrace this area of study at whatever age.

Yet there is still probably no aspect of the English curriculum which is less understood and where there is so much prejudice to overcome. Indeed, while this book was being written, a major political storm arose over the failure of the then government to publish the work which it had itself commissioned in the form of Professor Ronald Carter's Language in the National Curriculum (LINC) project. The fuss made in the popular press over this was both predictable and illuminating. In response to this John

Haynes (LINC co-ordinator in the South East Consortium) pointed out in a letter to the Times Educational Supplement (12 July 1991) that 'in the media "debate" about language, knowledge about language is inversely proportional to confidence in opinions about it.' Certainly, when I went at about the same time to see the Minister of State responsible for LINC (Tim Eggar) on behalf of an organization of English Tutors in University Departments of Education (ETUDE), I and my colleague were left in no doubt about the government's view. Parents, we were told, want their children to learn to read and spell correctly, and they are not interested in all these new-fangled notions about language which simply complicate and confuse where all is clear if we only stick with traditional ideas and values.

Yet the whole point of LINC was that it should enable teachers, amongst other things, to cope better with the task of helping children to read and spell, as well as providing them with the knowledge about language that is required in the light of the National Curriculum. The net result of the government's suppression of LINC has been to ensure more discussion of language issues in education in the second half of 1991 than ever before and it was against this background that the current volume was both commissioned and written.

I felt that there was still nothing available in an easily accessible form for the busy teacher which had the clarity and forcefulness of John Keen's earlier book, overtaken though it had been by many new developments in thinking about language education since it was first published. In asking him to bring his earlier work up-to-date I expected something that would provide precisely the basis for in-service education that LINC had been intended to provide and I knew that the book would grow out of John's own extensive experience in in-service work with teachers. In producing the present volume John has succeeded beyond my expectations. The book gradually builds upon the teacher's own developing confidence in his or her own understanding of language and, in the words of the title of one of its chapters, succeeds in 'placing language at the centre'. It is a humane and clear treatment of its subject which manages to provide a good deal of informative material within a short compass. It is, above all, essentially practical: there is no shortage here of actual examples of classroom work and plenty of ideas for what to do with language throughout the whole process of secondary education.

The book goes well beyond this simple brief, however. It provides a secure basis for teachers to develop their theoretical understanding in this area so that teachers of language world-wide can elaborate their work in this important area of study and understanding. When this book is published it will be just 21 years since the original publication of *Language in Use*. What Professor Halliday and his team started then has now come of age and 'linguistic science' has a firmly established and secure place in the English classroom. 1991 and 1992 has seen a remarkable profusion of books in this area after a relatively long neglect and John Keen's contribution is a signally important one.

Anthony Adams

Preface

This book is an attempt to share some experiences and ways of thinking about the place of language in English which developed out of my work with 11–16 and 16+ sixth form pupils in secondary comprehensive schools during the 1980s.

My debt to the pupils of JFS Comprehensive School in Camden, Knutsford County High School and Padgate County High School in Cheshire will become clear in the following pages. Thanks are also due to my colleagues at these schools, and most especially to Alec Shorrocks, Head of English at Knutsford School. I am also grateful to Richard Jones and to Nadine Hugoud for moral and practical support.

The author and publisher are grateful to the Joint Matriculation Board for permission to quote copyright material.

1 Building on language experience

Language study means the exploration of aspects of natural language in the context of some relevant theoretical framework. An example is this essay written by a 13-year-old pupil during a detention she had received for talking in class when she was supposed to be writing.

Talking

I think talking must be the most enjoyable and interesting thing out of everything I do. I can talk myself into things and out of things better than I can do anything.

Talking comes from your voice box in your throat, and I don't think it would be much of a life without a voice. I wouldn't be able to do anything if I lost mine. I wouldn't be able to tell disgusting jokes or talk about secrets and problems or find out what my friends have been doing or tell them to leave me alone. Talking is one of the main ways of communication, but teachers give us detentions, just for communicating.

Teachers say if you wrote as much as you talked you would be a genius, but you can talk a lot faster than you can write. If nobody could talk we probably wouldn't know anything.

What's wrong with making a nuisance of yourself by talking? It drives people mad, but that doesn't matter. It can't rot your teeth or kill anyone. It is completely harmless. Anyone who doesn't like talking is missing the best thing in the world.

Janine

Perhaps this committed and slyly critical apologia draws some of its effect from its composing voice; the cadence of 'I wouldn't be able to tell disgusting jokes ... or tell them to leave me alone'; the archly indignant 'teachers give us detentions, just for communicating'; the compressed logic which refutes 'if you wrote as much as you talked you would be a genius'. The tone with which Janine tries to initiate a dialogue between herself and her teacher on the issue of language is positive and enthusiastic, and although the metalanguage is limited to 'talk', 'write' and 'tell', the observations are accurate.

This pupil can deploy her knowledge about language to make a point; how can she be helped to develop and extend her understanding? To answer this question, we need a clearer idea of the issues she raises in her essay.

Janine already knows that talking is 'enjoyable and interesting ... the best thing in the world'. She knows that language can be used to persuade – 'I can talk myself into things' ... and to inform – 'talk about secrets'. She is aware of some of the social functions of language, such as 'telling jokes' and sharing problems. Her reference to 'your voice box in your throat' is a long way from the complexities of articulatory phonetics, but shows an encouraging sense of the physiological basis of language. Janine can set talking in wider theoretical frameworks; of communication with 'talking is one of the main ways of communication', and of *language and knowledge* with 'If nobody could talk we probably wouldn't know anything'. She is aware of the implications of the relationship between language and power, for instance that teachers set the agenda for language use in classrooms.

Her observations also suggest other questions.

Why is talking enjoyable and interesting for most people?
Why do so many people find writing less enjoyable and interesting?
What is the difference between persuading and informing?
How can language be used for persuading and for informing?
Are the social functions of language separate from its other purposes?
How does 'your voice box in your throat' create the sounds of language?
If 'talking is one of the main ways of communication', what are the other ways?
How is knowledge coded in language?
What kinds of knowledge does talking make available?
How does writing alter and extend available knowledge?
What limitations do social organizations place on the use of language?
What formal and functional differences are there between speaking and writing?

Following up these issues might also remind us that learning to talk is not just a matter of mastering the sound system, grammar and vocabulary of a language, but that a speaker also has to match language up with social situations and roles, to keep a purpose in mind, to compete with other speakers for a turn. The quality of speaking also depends on the nature of the whole interaction to which it contributes, one of the many factors which causes so much difficulty for teachers in trying to apply examination board criteria to GCSE students' oral work.

Some of the issues raised by Janine's essay can be investigated using available resources. The school or college may have access to a cross-sectional model of the vocal tract to illustrate some of the ways in which human speech sounds are produced. Pupils and students may be able to use their own knowledge and experience to build up a picture of different ways of communicating, including signs and symbols, gestures, codes, perhaps moving on to consider how animals communicate. A carefully worded questionnaire might be used to find out about schoolmates' attitudes to writing, in school and elsewhere. Other questions would need more preparation; investigating the differences between persuading and informing, perhaps using advertisements and promotional material, would require some rigorous definitions and a variety of examples.

Janine's essay represents a starting point in language study, and exploring some of the issues she raises helps to show how language study is a human discipline rooted in language experience which is itself composed of personal, attitudinal, emotional and social factors. Some approaches to language study in schools and colleges respect these personal and social bases, but many do not.

Some of the differences can be observed in the following two sets of comments about dialects and accents. The first sample consists of statements from some early GCE A Level English answers to examination questions for 16+ students about regional varieties of English. The second is a small selection of anecdotes from a class discussion by some 12-year-old pupils.

One of the most delicate problems in language study at all levels is how to exploit native speakers' intuitive understanding of language without also activating their linguistic prejudices. For example, it is a commonly held misunderstanding that regional dialects are in some way secondary, historically as well as in status and comprehensibility, to Standard English. So when students are required to define or characterize dialects, typical responses are as follows:

Sample 1

A Level English Language students' comments about dialects

- Dialects are variations of Standard English.
- Standard English is the basis of all the English dialects, which vary from it in different proportions and in different ways.
- Standard English is the foundation or centre of all other dialects.
- A lot of dialect comes from ignorance of Standard English.
- A dialect is a minor 'language' which has stemmed from a more important one.

From the point of view of language study, these statements are at best questionable, at worst inimical to objective and detailed investigation of this topic. Historically it is simply not the case that regional dialects developed out of a standard form. In fact, one widely accepted analysis is that one specific regional dialect developed for social and political reasons into a prestige and thence into a standard form. Linguistically, the claim that dialects are deviant forms of Standard English derives from a confusion between standard in the sense of *having widespread usage* and standard meaning *paradigmatic*, or operating as a reference from which other forms can be measured.

These students' comments contrast sharply with the following accounts from the personal experience of a Year 7 (11/12-year-olds) secondary class discussing times when they and people they knew had become aware of differences in accents and uses of words.

Sample 2

Year 7 pupils' comments on dialects and accents

Sarah

> I was born in Sheffield and – then we moved down to Norfolk – and – we'd been there five years then we had to move up – and I – I – didn't know what to say – really – I couldn't say the things I wanted to say because – I – I thought I'd say it wrong.

Susan

> My sister's friend you see – and she comes from – she comes from a different place – and she's got a funny accent and they're all trying to get her to talk how they did – and she – she's talking how they did but she – had to think about what she was saying because she wasn't too sure how to say it.

Scott

> Well – I've lived – I was born in London – till I was one so I didn't exactly pick up a lot of the accent then but – I – then I moved up to the ur – in the middle of the country and I lived there for – till I was four – and I got the accent then – and – when I moved up here – it was a bit of a shock but – I've got a bit of the accent – that's from here.

Lindsey

> There was this girl from our school called Anna-Marie and – she came from London and she used to go 'I come from London' (/'l^n'd^n/) and we always used to take the mick out of her.

Andrew

> My cousin comes from Yorkshire and – she used to say 'give up' instead of 'stop it' – we used to tease her about it.

Sarah's account shows that she understands from experience that the communicative problems between dialect speakers occur more from nervousness internalized from social pressure than from absolute mutual unintelligibility. This idea is confirmed by Susan's account, which also demonstrates the stultifying effects on speakers of their need to monitor their speech in unfamiliar linguistic situations. Lindsey and Andrew are aware of the very small linguistic differences which can become hugely significant in social terms, and of some of the particular ways in which peer group pressure can be applied to those who speak differently from the community norm.

The main differences between these two sets of comments relate first to their level of generality and secondly to their usefulness for exploring language. In Sample 1, students were unable, for a variety of reasons, to connect their view of language to their own felt experiences of talking with others, so in order to lay a basis for them to investigate language, they would need first to unlearn conceptual confusions. The steps taken by the second group of students are much more modest; they simply recount, at first or second hand, their experiences. But within these accounts are encoded the seeds of a theoretical framework – peer group pressure, monitoring, socially diagnostic language uses – which can offer a principled basis for genuine language study.

Nearly everyone has an anecdote about accents and dialects to contribute to the pool of experience. One striking example, from a mature A Level English Language student who was willing to start from language experience rather than folk linguistics, shows how linguistic snobbery too has its inverted version:

> Having lived in the far south of the UK for two years, I moved to a city in the North of England. On my first day at junior school I said to the girl next to me, 'Does your mummy make your sandwiches for you?' She replied, 'I haven't gorra mummy, I've gorra mam.' I didn't speak very much after that until I managed to acquire a local accent and the slang of my age group.

If its relation to language experience is the key to the place of language study on the English curriculum, it is on just this ground that language study most requires careful justification. For example, why not simply develop language experience and leave language study to the academics? Surely it is more important for young people to be able to read and understand a variety of texts and to express themselves clearly and effectively in speech and writing. On this argument, it may occasionally be necessary to step back and look at this or that aspect of language – discussing the morphology of a complex word to assist progress in spelling, working out the underlying structure of some problematic text, looking up the history of some key term to illuminate a literary passage. But these are *ad hoc* and pragmatic, minor diversions from the broad path of language development. To take the argument a step further, it might be said that systematic attempts to make explicit observations on the language of texts, or to explore the nature of the language system which underlies speaking and writing merely adds an unnecessary, and potentially confusing, dimension to what pupils have to assimilate.

If this were so, the advocates of curricular language study have to show that there was a possibility of feedback between pupils' explicit understanding about language and their ability to use language. It was precisely the realization that no transfer of competence between formal grammar teaching and written expression takes place which ousted the topic from its place on the English curriculum. The same objections which led to the rejection of parsing and clause analysis seem to apply equally to any explicit study of language use: that they have no beneficial effects on children's written expression; that they alienate pupils from their own real use of language; that most 11–16-year-olds cannot cope with the concepts; that the simple-minded descriptive categories available travesty the infinite expressive potential of language.

In any case, if we take grammar as the most dramatic case of an aspect of language study which has been tried but failed, developments in linguistics this century have shown how inadequate school grammars were as descriptive frameworks for English. Worse still, linguistics has produced a plethora of competing grammatical theories, each with its own assumptions, distinctions and definitions. If this confusion is equally true of the rest of language theory, how would it be possible to avoid irremediable confusion in our classrooms?

The one axiom of language theory that is generally agreed, that all forms and uses of language are equal in linguistic complexity and communicative potential, runs counter to the intuitions of teachers who are constantly faced with questions of priority and judgement. Being able to assume that all uses of language are equally valid is very important if language theory is to take its place as a systematic discipline, but it does not translate easily into curricular terms, seeming as it does to reduce literature to one aspect of language use among many, thus alienating the many literature-trained teachers whose main motivation is to share important and valuable language experiences gained from poems, plays and novels.

Against all this, there seems to be a consensus that language is a theme of all other aspects of learning, that language is as much a part of the human environment as the institutions studied in history or the physical environment studied in geography; that language mediates large parts of our emotional, social and intellectual experience, that language is somehow significant in promoting the kind of tolerance and understanding without which education reduces to socialization.

Language is the first and most significant of every child's intellectual accomplishments. By giving language an appropriate place on the curriculum we are tacitly recognizing this achievement, and offering automatic but well-founded esteem as the starting point for learning.

Language also offers opportunities for bridging the gap between school and non-school experience – school and home, school and peer group, school and sub-culture, a gap so often destructive of esteem and curiosity. If we use and extend this experience through discussion and personal narrative, we can ensure that pupils' study of language is not alienating or conceptually beyond their reach. The possibility of coherence across pupils' school experience may also be offered through the forum of language study. Language Across the Curriculum was supercurricular, a subject without a home; language study, in its rightful place – firmly on the English curriculum, subsumes language across the curriculum within the more general issue of how language is used by people in schools.

Language study is also important because language is for living as well as for learning. Being able to use language effectively may improve life chances, and might enhance the quality of experiences, but it doesn't necessarily help someone to understand how they are being linguistically manipulated by politicians, advertisers, pundits, propagandists and justifiers of the unjustifiable. That needs a cooler, more detached stance, and some ability to recognize purposes and their means of realization.

The educational justification for language study is that, perhaps more than any other discipline, it allows learners to engage in the crucial process of detachment without losing a sense of the full weight and richness of the language experience which must, as a matter of logic, constitute the starting point for exploration. The problem for teachers then becomes how to develop and extend students' and pupils' natural responses to language.

It is a mistake to think that these responses must always be at the higher levels of explicitness. Very often the early stages of language awareness will consist in pupils bringing some part of their fund of understanding to a commonly understood aspect of language use through anecdote or narrative. For example, the following account developed out of a Year 9 class's exploration of what happens when people spread information, ideas and opinions by word of mouth. The first examples to emerge were such favourites as the transformation of 'Send for artillary; we're going to advance' into the less than martial request, 'Send for our Hilary; we're going to a dance', moving on to personal experiences of occasions when messages had been misinterpreted. Some spectacular results emerged when groups worked together to try out what happens when exaggeration, speculation and confusion are brought to bear on such everyday events as

- Christine burnt her toast this morning
- One of the teachers was seen buying a pair of shoelaces last Saturday
- Millie had the measles so she was off school
- Jane went on holiday to Spain for a week
- Julie went for a meal with her family on her birthday.

One of the written narratives to emerge from this process was based on a minor domestic incident:

The rumour

'Ricky trapped his finger in the door,' said his mum to her neighbour. 'Ricky broke his fingers in an accident,' said the next door neighbour to her friend. 'Ricky had an accident,' the friend said to her husband. 'Guess what,' said the neighbour's friend's husband to his workmate, 'Ricky was in quite a serious accident.'

'What happened to him?' he asked.

'Well I think he's in hospital, so it must be serious.'

Everyone wanted to be the bearer of the exclusive news so they told their own story.

The workman's mate told his wife who told her friend. 'Ricky is on the edge of death after quite a bad accident. Might be fatal you know.' They chatted on, oohing and aahing about this fatal accident.

'Ricky has been killed in an accident,' she told her son. 'It was a car, on the motorway I think.'

The neighbour's friend's husband's workmate's wife's son picked up the phone.

'Hello, Ricky,' he said. 'Apparently you've just been killed in a motorway accident.'

'No,' smiled Ricky, 'It's just a rumour.'

The familiar classroom activity of writing stories provided a secure framework for this pupil to hold in character, action and language forms some of the general ideas about language he had been exploring with his classmates during the previous lessons. At the same time, he had enabled himself to move his own language development forward by finding an appropriate narrative structure to build up to the climax and finish in bathos. The pupil's relish for language, fostered by discussion and roleplay, emerges most strikingly in the way he closes the narrative circle by his daring characterization of Ricky's friend as 'The neighbour's friend's husband's workmate's wife's son'.

The distinction between *using language* and *knowing about language* is a useful heuristic for the early stages of curriculum planning. But this example suggests that it may be more profitable to think in terms of overlapping and interacting levels of explicitness. So we can understand pupils' language competence and their explicit understanding of language as having a place on a wide continuum, ranging from low to high levels of explicitness. At the low end is implicit knowledge of language as it emerges in language acts; for example, the ability to use an informal tone to a friend and a formal tone to a stranger, or to recognize when a speaker has made a mistake. At the high end is Linguistics, with its formal and rigorous methodology covering all aspects of language, and assuming a distinction between discourse and the abstract language system which underlies speech acts. In between, at different levels of explicitness, are Language Awareness, focusing on certain key areas of discourse which can be used as starting points for exploration, and Language Study, employing more systematic methods for making explicit the basis of key language systems.

Relations between the levels on this continuum can be judged from a 15-minute discussion of *slang* by a class of Year 8 pupils in a mixed-ability class in a comprehensive school. The issue had arisen while a group of pupils had been reading each other's stories. Some pupils had observed the use of what they termed 'slang' in one story, and the writer had denied that the expression was slang. The problem of definition thus arose in a quite natural way. I took the opportunity to give the whole class a chance to think the problem through, and wrote four questions on the blackboard:

Slang

What is slang?
Why do we use slang?
Where do slang words come from?
Who uses slang words?

These questions were on view to the class during the discussion, and offered a kind of informal agenda. The transcript starts a little way into the discussion.

Discussion on 'slang'

Pupil 1: can you – use slang to cover up a word that you
Teacher: use slang for?
Pupil 1: a cover-up
Teacher: a cover-up – how do you mean?
Pupil 1: like – when you want to – say something – say you use slang instead to say it so other people don't know what you're saying
Teacher: oh that's good – let's develop that idea – Janice says that sometimes you use slang words so that other people – don't know what you're saying – anyone think of an example of that – or – how that works – or
Pupil 2: it makes – it might make other people laugh – some people find it funny
Teacher: yeah they might do – that's – that's not quite the same point as Janice's though is it
Pupil 3: [inaudible]
Teacher: yes – explain that a bit
Pupil 3: well – you change – you write it down and you change the – the last word to the first word – the third letter – ur – do it again – and if it doesn't sound right you muddle some words round so that it sounds good
Teacher: so it's like talking in code isn't it – yeah – any others
Pupil 4: I've just thought of one – ur – like ur – naff
Teacher: naff yeah for
Pupil 3: biff – biff
Teacher: biff – yeah – was that good or bad?
Pupil 3: biff – biff – bad
Pupil 4: bad – yeah
Teacher: trying to hide things and cover them up – yes
Pupil 5: sir if someone calls you a name you don't know whether it's good or bad
Teacher: yeah – just as I don't know whether some of these words are good or bad –
Pupil 6: just – can I just say – go back to what Janice said – someone calls you – if you call someone something – bad – you think it's bad –

and they say – aw what ur – why did you call me – something bad –
I don't like that – and he clobbers you one or something – and then
you can say aw why did you hit me – I was saying ur how – how
nice you were – or something

Teacher: yeah because people don't know what the word means – good point
Clare – Angie

Pupil 7:   um dough for money and cops for police

Teacher: yeah dough for money and cops for police

Pupil 8:   dosh

Teacher: dosh

Pupil 6:   the old bill

Teacher: the old bill for the police

Pupil 5:   smackers

Pupil 11:   for pounds

Pupil 9:   sheets for money

Pupil 10:   a ton is a hundred pounds – a grand – megaspondoolies is a lot of
money

Teacher: lovely word – megaspondoolies is a beautiful word isn't it – any more

Pupil 11:   bucks for dollars

Pupil 7:   a tidy – for – for a lot of money

Pupil 3:   a squid

Teacher: a squid?

Pupil 3:   yeah – like – here's that sick squid I owe you

[groans from the class]

Pupil 5:   you change words because they're boring as well

Pupil 3:   yeah they do –

Pupil 6:   the nick

Teacher: yeah – nicked is *You've been arrested* – nick is the jail

Pupil 5:   the clink

Pupil 9:   the slammer

Pupil 11:   the cooler

Pupil 3:   porridge

Pupil 6:   the screws

Teacher: now – I could have filled the board with these couldn't I – now –
going back to Janice's point – why are there so many – so many
hundreds of words for things to do with money – the law police –

Pupil 5:   maybe some people didn't like some of the ones people came out with

Pupil 6:   they're secret words so the police can't – so that people can warn
each other

Pupil 7:   without them – without the police being able to understand

Pupil 6:   and people all get used to the same words – and if they use the same
words everyone'll be able to understand what they're saying – or –
or – or the authorities get to know the meaning

Pupil 3:   if you switch something – and somebody else doesn't know the
code – you can talk and they won't know what you're on about

Pupil 7:   so you have to keep changing them – the word

Pupil 10:   people – just made up one word – and words just developed from
that one

Pupil 11: sir you get like – in words from different areas – like – say an area's famous for something and you all make up words for doing it – different areas have different ways of words – and it sounds dead old-fashioned to be using words ages ago – they sometimes make up old languages – like – ur sago language

Teacher: sago language

Pupil 6: jam sandwich

Pupil 5: handles

Teacher: why do we use slang at all?

Pupil 5: it's interesting

Pupil 11: sir because you – people don't want to sound dead posh like Queen's English and if you say like that sounds snobby – you make up – other words

Teacher: so if you want to sound more casual

Pupil 11: yeah

Pupil 10: giving more expression to things

Teacher: yeah expressing yourself

Pupil 5: it's different – makes you different

Teacher: do we have any ideas – where do slang words come from – someone said that someone just invents them – but where else might they come from – Jo

Pupil 12: you sometimes watch these films and – say like – someone says *You're nicked*

Pupil 13: like *wag it* on Grange Hill

Pupil 11: someone goes like – a foreign language – and they think ur – that word sounds good – I think I'll use it

Pupil 5: well – but these words on television – well they must have got it from somewhere as well

Teacher: yeah – good point that Barry – I like the one about foreign languages though – anyone know any words that come from foreign languages – any slang words

Pupil 6: kaput

Teacher: kaput?

Pupil 6: it's broken in German – it's the proper word for broken in German

Pupil 4: gremlin

Teacher: what language is that from?

Pupil 4: it's probably from – the war

Pupil 3: the war – it's got passed over

Pupil 7: zatso – comes from America

Pupil 10: critter

Teacher: yeah – it's the American pronunciation of creature isn't it – it's actually the old *English* pronunciation of creature too – that's how we used to pronounce it

Pupil 3: they get passed round

Pupil 11: when people go abroad – like you go to Australia and you come back calling everyone sport – like – sorry sport

Pupil 7: from penfriends – friends

Pupil 13: round the country

Teacher: who uses slang words the most
Pupil 10:   young people
Teacher: how's that
Pupil 10:   well – you wouldn't hear old people going Let's have a boogie and all that
Teacher: might do – but fair point
Pupil 11:   younger ones – ur – more likely to do it because they're bringing in new words but older people are used to the type they used to use – they keep with those rather than pick up some of the ones their children are using
Pupil 6:   I think – ur – a few – if you take – a few decades ago – it would be males because women used to be thought of as – really elegant people but – I think now it's become more – more equal than it used to be – so – generally – boys and girls use it
Teacher: elegant
Pupil 5:   older people are from a different generation so they're not going to be using our words are they
Teacher: that's right – older people – older people have their own slang words don't they – that's right
Pupil 14:   older people use it the most because – when you're kids you get told off for saying it but nobody says – tells the adults off for saying it
Teacher: so nobody can tell them off – Clare
Pupil 6:   I think the teenagers do because – all the mums – they're too old for our kind of language
Teacher: yeah
Pupil 6:   they're up to – they go *Oh when I was a child there wasn't words like this* and stuff like that
Teacher: well I can tell you that there was – your mums and dads had their own slang when they were younger – yes go on
Pupil 1:   um I think everybody uses it
Teacher: maybe children seem to use more but – what do you think Mike
Pupil 11:   well – it's not the case with my dad – because I – I'm always saying slang words and he copies them – and – he's got every single one I've had and he's always using the old ones and the new ones
Teacher: the old ones and the new ones together?
Pupil 11:   yeah – so he's always gone round like that
Teacher: so – how's that sound to you
Pupil 11:   sounds really weird
Teacher: yeah I'll bet it does
Pupil 6:   it's more children kind of – teenagers than
Teacher: yeah
Pupil 6:   my brother tries to – when my brother goes to work – he always uses like really funny words and when he brings them home – and I – I – me and my brother can really pick them up really easy and we can say them dead well – and my dad tries to say it and he's – when he's trying – when he's – when you slide all the words into one – you go – and he can't say it at all – but he tries to –

Teacher: I wonder why that is
Pupil 6:   he just can't get the – the rhythm of the words
Pupil 9:   yeah my dad – when I say a slang word in front of my dad he
        doesn't mind it but he tries to copy it and he always says it in the
        wrong – sort of way
Teacher: yeah – that's right
Pupil 7:   I do – my mum does – it doesn't sound right – she might hear it
        wrong – or she just – she knows the words but she doesn't
Pupil 6:   the wrong sense – she uses it in the wrong sense
Pupil 7:   in the wrong way
Teacher: so adults have the same problem learning your slang as you have in
        learning the kind of official vocabulary
Pupil 6:   sometimes they just give up
Teacher: yeah – yeah they do
Pupil 5:   sir the sound of the words can change it completely – like if you say
        Oh well done or if you say Oh well done – it means two completely
        different things – like when you're sarcastic
Teacher: yes right – you've got to pick up the right tone
Pupil 15:   my brother – we were walking up – and he was going – like big bum
        big bum like this – and he can get away with it and when I say
        anything to my brother – I get – I get into trouble a lot
Teacher: do you find that – that boys can get away with more bad words than
        girls can
Pupil 4:   yes because girls – there's not supposed to be as many girls
        swearing – it doesn't sound right if girls swear anyway
Pupil 3:   no it doesn't
Pupil 6:   well girls are meant to be dead ladylike but –
Teacher: but what Clare
Pupil 6:   but they're not
[bell rings]

The class is thinking aloud about language, with little conscious attempt to structure an overall argument. Pupils draw on examples from their own language experience, and, towards the end of the discussion, on the subtleties of their understanding about language in their own families, in the form of anecdotes. Yet most of the discussion is at a surprisingly general level, and at various points the participants cooperate in developing logical arguments and explanations of a range of linguistic phenomena.

As is the nature of this kind of free-ranging discussion, some issues are made fully explicit, while many others are touched on and left, perhaps for a later time. In response to the teacher's requests for open explanations rather than personal experiences, pupils try to formulate what amount to socio-linguistic explanations for certain kinds of slang usage, in terms of hidden or 'secret' meanings. The early suggestion by Pupil 1 that one of the functions of slang is to mask communication to outsiders, developed as 'talking in code', given tentative exemplification in Pupil 3's rather confused character-ization of a cipher, and Pupil 6's example of someone mischievously using an esoteric term as an insult, linked with Pupil 7's catalytic examples of 'dough' and 'cops', leads to a rich vein of examples of terms which originated in underworld slang, and to the complex logic of Pupils 3, 6 and 7 in developing an explanation of why some slang words change so quickly.

It is worth analysing in some detail how this exchange builds on and refines ideas from the preceding parts of the discussion.

> *Pupil 6:* they're secret words so the police can't – so that people can warn each other

Pupil 6 had already shown her ability to think in semi-realized narrative, and had established that language can be used for devious purposes, in her point about slyly insulting someone. She had also offered three examples of terms from the relevant semantic field in the build-up to this statement – 'the old bill', 'the nick', 'the screws'. In this case, the collocation of 'police' and 'warn' suggests that she may have an unspoken script in mind involving a group of criminals trying to communicate in the presence of the police. Her use of the general 'people' suggests that she wants to allow for the possibility of generalizing her point to wider social situations.

> *Pupil 7:* without them – without the police being able to understand

Pupil 7 is the group's synthesizer. Her self-assigned role is to follow up, re-state and make explicit the implications behind other pupils' suggestions. Though she says very little in the discussion as a whole, there is evidence that she follows its course very closely. For example, her initial examples of slang words – 'um dough for money and cops for police' – is intended as a response to the teacher's request for an example of slang as 'a cover-up'. In this case, reference to 'the police ...' offers empathy with Pupil 6's half-realized scenario, and refers the example back to Pupil 1's original idea, that 'you use slang words so that other people – don't know what you're saying'.

> *Pupil 6:* and people all get used to the same words – and if they use the same words everyone'll be able to understand what they're saying – or – or – or the authorities get to know the meaning

This is the heart of the argument: if 'secret words' do not change frequently, they cease to be secret. Pupil 6 again uses a hypothetical general scenario as the main vehicle for thinking the issue through. This time Pupil 6 has re-solved one problem related to the supposed participants; 'police' was useful to stimulate an imaginative reconstruction, but Pupil 6 can see that the idea of 'secret words' has a more general application. Hence 'the authorities' are identified as the superordinate term.

> *Pupil 3:* if you switch something – and somebody else doesn't know the code – you can talk and they won't know what you're on about

Pupil 3's 'sick squid' shows his interest in wordplay, and here he is developing his own earlier idea of codes created by changing letters in written messages. His use of 'switch' instead of the more general 'change' and his explicit use of the word 'code', picked up from the teacher's comment on his account of writing a coded message, both contribute to a very clear statement about how the principle of codes applies to the uses of slang under discussion.

Pupil 3's contribution restates a part of Pupil 6's argument, presenting it in a different way. His special contribution is a new focus on the third part; he makes the important point that the 'secret' communication system only works if the 'authorities' don't know the code.

Pupil 7: so you have to keep changing them – the word

Pupil 7 draws the final, explicit conclusion which lines this neat series of logical inferences against the original question, as stated by the teacher, of why there are so many different slang terms related to the law.

The pupils' willingness to pick up an issue and explore it in a variety of ways is shown too in their responses to the issue of who uses slang words. The question of what effect speaker, hearer and overhearer might have on the development of slang terms emerges early in the discussion, and the pupils then focus energetically on gender and generation. The discussion culminates in a series of five anecdotes, from Pupils 11, 6, 9, 7 and 15, related to family experience and showing some features of the generation and gender divisions which can be indexed by how key colloquial terms are used. Pupil 6 and Pupil 7 again offer significant points, Pupil 6 on how adults find difficulty in acquiring the phonology of new words, and Pupil 7 on similar problems with their semantics and usage.

It is worth listing some of the main social and linguistic issues which the pupils raise in this part of the discussion:

Younger speakers as a major source of new words.

Changing roles and perceptions of female speakers.

Adult responses to younger speakers' use of 'slang'.

The assumption of a form of language closely associated with younger speakers – 'our words', 'our kind of language'.

The perceived incongruity of juxtaposed words associated with different generations.

The importance of rhythm and tone in identifying the social significance of certain words.

The metalinguistic terms used by pupils in this discussion include: 'write', 'word', 'letter', 'a name', 'call someone something', 'what the word means', 'old language', 'sago language', 'sound dead posh', 'Queen's English', 'more expression', 'a foreign language', 'the proper word', 'new words', 'our words', 'our kind of language', 'slang words', 'funny words', 'secret words', 'warn', 'understand', 'the same words', 'saying,' 'the meaning,' 'the rhythm of the words', 'the wrong sense', 'the sound of the words', 'sarcastic', 'it doesn't sound right', 'swear', 'switch' (= substitute), 'code', 'talk', 'on about'. They are not particularly technical, though as far as these pupils are concerned some of them have senses specifically refined for this discussion; these include 'secret words', 'switch', 'code'. Of course, classroom time is too precious to insist that pupils continually reinvent concepts for which there are already adequate terms. But this discussion does show that, given sympathetic and challenging circumstances, pupils can develop a vocabulary for talking, and thinking, about language without the mediation of a complex layer of imposed technical terms, and, more importantly, that they can deploy that vocabulary in seeking to understand linguistic principles.

In exploring this range of language issues, the pupils constantly allude to the lower levels of explicitness – schoolmates using language to play tricks on each other, criminals planning activities within earshot of the police by using argot, the dialogue of films and TV programmes, parents' attempts to imitate the slang of their offspring.

There is constant interplay between the pupils' speculating, hypothesizing, explaining, exemplifying about language, and the language experience which they draw on. If this discussion were placed on the implicit – explicit continuum suggested earlier in this chapter, it would lie mostly in the language awareness region, with considerable reference to language use, and perhaps an excursion into language study, for example with Pupils 3, 6 and 7's explanation of why slang words change so quickly.

An impressionistic mapping of the main elements of the discussion onto this schema might look as follows:

Elements of discussion at three levels of explicitness

Language Use	*Language Awareness*	*Language Study*
	Pupil 1's idea of slang as 'a cover-up'	
Pupil 3's 'code'	*Examples*: 'biff', 'naff', 'dough', 'cops', 'screws'	
Pupil 6's example of calling names	*Examples*: 'dough', 'cops', the 'screws'	Pupils 3, 6, 7's 'secret words' explanation
	Pupil 11's ideas about regional forms and not sounding 'posh'	
Pupils 12 and 13's references to films and TV	*Examples of loan words*: e.g. kaput	
	Pupils 5, 11 and 14's discussion of whether older or younger speakers use more slang	
Pupils 6, 7, 9, 11 and 15's anecdotes about parents' attempts to use slang	Some explicit comments on key points; e.g. Pupil 5's identification of tone as a key semantic marker	

As long as the topic is worthwhile, this kind of discussion, involving as it does processes of hypothesizing, formulating, synthesizing, will always contribute to the language and personal development of participants. However, there may also be ways in which the teacher can facilitate continued development. If the aim is to further explicit understanding of the linguistic bases of use of slang, then pupils might be encouraged to translate language awareness into language study, perhaps by a more systematic exploration of issues covered in discussion at the 'awareness' level – the use of slang across generations, for example. This work might take the form of an empirical survey of what speakers of different generations understand by each other's 'slang' terms. If it is appropriate, the aim might be to use the general ideas generated by discussion to feed back into aspects of language development more directly related to language use. In this case, for example, a class might use the idea of slang terms related to the law coupled with the theme of 'secret words' as a starting point for roleplay or narrative. Ideally, the development should move both ways; implicit language experience becomes the ground for the more explicit language awareness, and ideas and principles from language awareness offer themes for language activities.

With some topics, such as slang, the gap between language experience and language study may be narrow enough for pupils and students to be able to exploit their experience-based intuitions with comparative ease. The dangers of moving them too quickly into the higher levels of explicitness become more evident in considering some of the areas where the crucial gap is wider.

While the concept of *levels of explicitness* provides a helpful theoretical basis for thinking about programmes of study, it is not necessarily a reliable chronological framework. Language experience brings with it an element of language awareness, as the pupils' anecdotes about accent and dialect quoted earlier demonstrate. Neither is language awareness always a necessary condition for language study; it is possible, though it might not be desirable, to engage in grammatical or semantic analysis without reference to a social, personal or interactional context.

It may be sensible to think of experience, awareness and study as modes which provide the principles for developmental phases rather than as stages of development. This implies that all three modes will be present at any one time in language-based activities; only the emphasis will differ at different levels of development. The concerns of language theorists and of teachers wishing to develop language awareness programmes are related, but there are differences. Linguistics distinguishes very sharply between *competence* and *performance*, i.e. between actual utterances and the abstract system of rules, tendencies and relationships which underlie exchanges, texts and discourses. In language awareness we take performance, that is, utterances and texts, rather than abstract systems as the starting point. In this way, pupils are encouraged to understand language from the inside, from the point of view of expert users, with language treated as part of the logic of experience, and factors such as moral responsibility, relationships, group and personal identity taken into account. The principle being argued for here, in brief, is that awareness of discourse should take priority over the study of formal factors in language awareness.

This does no more than reflect intuitive responses to texts and utterances. Even in texts in which formal factors, such as grammar and lexis, are foregrounded through deviation or markedness, we assume that the text has a valid discourse function. For example, the following text was the English language version of the back of a ticket for entry to a National Park in Spain. It was also printed in German and French as well as Spanish.

> *Visitors will be requested*
> – Not in the National Park damage trees and bushes and not pluck flowers
> – Not in the caves touch stalactites
> – Not light fire
> – Not throw rubbish around
> – Not walk off pathways and roads
> – Obey to the keeper's guidances
> *It is forbidden*
> – Bathing in the reservations
> – Let dogs loose in the open
> – Carry arms
> – Fishing and hunting without permission
> *This ticket is valuable for one visit to the National Park during three days at the most*

The academic linguist might want to investigate the deviations from Standard English grammar, in particular the non-finite verb forms and the use of prepositions, as well as some of the semantic oddities, such as 'the keeper's guidances', 'the reservations' and 'this ticket is valuable'. But pupils and students at earlier stages of language development might profit more by using the cross-linguistic context as a stimulus for investigating the varieties and functions of notices and warnings, perhaps by collecting examples from their own environment, or by devising their own, and discussing who they are for, who has the right to issue them, where they are to be found, whether they are taken seriously.

A further stage might be to consider the wording of public notices and warnings, and whether this is appropriate for its purposes and readers. For example, would you be more or less likely to follow the instructions on your National Park ticket if you have to think a little harder to work out exactly what they mean? As a way of exploring some of these issues with a Year 8 class, I gave redrafted copies of a county council article to a class a few weeks before the end of the summer term and asked them to think about different ways of warning young people and their parents about the dangers of swimming in canals. The text we used was as follows:

Canal danger

A water safety campaign has reminded young people and their parents of the dangers of canals.

A spokesperson said, 'Canal banks can be very slippery, and some of them are overgrown with trees and undergrowth.'

'Canal water can be deeper than you might think, and there are sudden variations in depth in some places, with surprisingly cold water and dangerous currents close to lock gates. The hidden dangers include broken bottles, rubbish such as rusty bicycles and weeds.'

'We know that some children like playing near canals, especially during school holidays, and accidents can so easily happen as a result.'

'We would warn children not to play unsupervised near canals, and appeal to them to use their local swimming baths instead.'

As part of a display which was mounted just before the summer holidays, the pupils created posters embellished with memorable slogans, wrote letters to parents, composed edifying stories for younger children, and created booklets for their schoolmates. From the point of view of language development, the class enhanced their awareness of the importance of audience, redrafted to find a tone for their letters to parents which was serious without being alarmist, and learnt the importance of crafting a structure for their leaflets which built up enough information and sensible advice to give real force to the explicit warning and appeals which they intended should stay in their readers' memories.

The success of this short project encouraged me to develop a wider module on warnings to use with other classes in the following school year. So in addition to the *Canal Danger* project, my Year 8 groups discussed verbal and non-verbal warnings, including examples from animal communication, and from road signs. We used Jenny Joseph's poem *Warning* as a starting point for exploring how clothes – 'I shall wear purple/With a red hat ... /And satin sandals' – and behaviour – 'I shall ... pick the flowers in other people's gardens/And learn to spit' – can communicate non-verbally. We built up a stock of examples of various warnings, including these:

- Trespassers will be prosecuted.
- ... *or else*.
- **DANGER: 10,000 volts.**
- Anything you say may be taken down and used in evidence against you in a court of law.
- Lighthouses.
- Deep End 12m.
- A selection of road signs from the Highway Code.
- Examples of birdsongs used to signal territories.
- Examples of animals using sound, colour, posture to deter predators and rivals.

We discussed what different ways there were of making sure the warnings were communicated clearly, how many different channels of communication were used, how some of the culture-bound warnings, such as '... *or else*' might be explained to someone unfamiliar with this message, and we thought about the philosophical problem of distinguishing between a warning and a threat. We tried to sum up the discussion with a chart of the contexts, audiences and channels for some of our examples:

Warning	Place or situation	Type of danger or problem	Who the warning is meant for	Verbal or non-verbal	Written or spoken

Having spent several lessons on relatively abstract language study work, however pupil centred and activity-based, and being constrained by the disciplines of various kinds of transactional writing, we also wanted to use the general ideas we had explored as a resource for language development through narrative writing. Accordingly, we constructed treatments and suggestions for stories which included a warning in some form. The result was a selection of lively adventure stories, many involving lighthouses and high-voltage pylons, some explorations of human relations ('I warned you about Jonathan ...'), and this account from one pupil who had tried to feed into his narrative some of what he had learnt about the variety of different kinds of warning:

So heed my warning

'Oooh! My leg! If only I could give it a scratch, but with all this plaster on, all I get is irritation,' David complained. 'Tut, speaking of irritation, here comes Steve.' David's older brother entered the feebly decorated ward and exclaimed, 'Greetings, oh mighty single-legged one, and how are you?'

'I couldn't be better, my wise and loyal brother,' David replied, attempting to match his brother's wit.

'Well, that's nice to hear, but not all news is nice I'm afraid. Mum is coming in twenty minutes, meaning that you must explain how you broke your leg. But we could make a deal. For a certain proportion of your pocket money you can have a specially prepared speech which should get you out of trouble.'

'Not this time, Steve. Mum must know the truth.'

'OK then, wriggle out of this one, explaining to mum that you broke your leg while exploring a shack near a river which is known to be strictly out of bounds, and that you fell through its roof. Bye, bruv, and good luck.' Steve went off laughing.

David rolled over onto his back and started to doze off, drowned in thoughts of what would happen if he told his mother the truth. His mother's face appeared to be floating above him. Steve leaned over her shoulder smirking. 'I want an explanation,' his mum was demanding.

'Well,' David began, 'I went down to the river and began to follow it until I came to a large wire fence. On it a sign said, "Trespassers will be prosecuted". It meant nothing to me at the time, so I climbed over the fence and followed the river, as before. But on my travels I came across an old shack. I began to explore it, and found a rotten ladder. With this I climbed onto the shack's rickety roof and of course it fell through. And that's why I'm here with a broken leg.'

'Why you little ... . You mean to say that you broke into private property? Why, how many times have I warned you? I've a good mind to ... .'

David woke up sweating. Suddenly mum entered the ward. 'David, how did this happen?'

David thought, double checked his thoughts, and made up his mind. 'Didn't I tell you I'd been offered a trial with the local rugby club ... ?'

2 Placing language at the centre

The case against placing language awareness at the centre of the English curriculum rests partly on the view that explication encourages a mechanistic version of language, and partly on the claim that alternative approaches make it unnecessary. Dennis Carter, in an essay on the individual nature of language and cultural development (1988), offers an example and a statement of principle:

> ... nine-year-old twins, one girl, one boy ... came into my class from another school on the opposite side of the country. She was bright, lively and good at getting things right. If I'd taught to an English programme with an 11+ assessment test, she would have registered a high score. Her brother, on the other hand, was lazy, acted silly and sat there grinning when referred to. The test would have condemned his English. Two children, from the same womb at the same time, arrived in my class as diverse a pair of children as could be imagined. True to expectations, the girl began to succeed in my class and the boy to fail. During our walks, however, new things began to emerge about the twins. Out of school in field or village the boy was animated. It was a common practice for the children to settle down and write about objects and places of their own choice. This became a much loved activity. The girl soon got cracking and produced pleasant little pieces very quickly. The boy would stand staring at things for long periods. Was he being lazy? Was he confirming all the reports, written and spoken, that had arrived in his wake like messages of doom? This was quite clearly not the case from the very first walk when he wrote:

> *Kissing-gate*

> Along by the kissing gate
> surrounded by nettles,
> blackberries are kissed
> by tempted wanderers
> for their lips are dark
> and also delicious

Dennis Carter goes on to comment more generally:

> Language develops most effectively and richly in children out of relationships
> of trust in open-ended contexts. As has been demonstrated here, children are
> quite capable of handling even the more sophisticated and intellectually chal-
> lenging ideas in their culture. They are also fully able to listen to and re-use
> the language that contains these ideas.

The boy's poem is sensuous and freshly observed, the example compelling.
Dennis Carter's conclusion derives from a similar source – active observation
and trust in his own experience. On the basis of this evidence it is impossible
not to share the author's apprehensions about the blight of a programmatic
curriculum driven by a graded national assessment framework. Yet a problem remains, mentioned by Dennis Carter, but not developed in his essay:
'The girl soon got cracking and produced pleasant little pieces very quickly'.
We cannot know whether any of the sister's 'pleasant little pieces' may have
been 'contributions to English culture', but having read many pieces from
pupils and students of the kind that Dennis Carter is referring to we know
that it is unlikely.

Roger Knight has argued on the basis of such examples that the 'knowledge about language' best suited to foster 'growth of language, of understanding, imagination, and skill' is that typified by poetry, and quotes HMI
in *Teaching Poetry in the Secondary School* as recommending 'prolonged
immersion in the reading of poetry'. Assimilating and deploying the store
of works and words is left to the operation of the 'cultural tradition',
characterized by Knight's quoting of Leavis as: 'a collaboratively sustained
reality in the way exemplified by a living language – by the language of
Shakespeare, of Blake and of Dickens'.

The problem for Dennis Carter and Roger Knight is that sometimes
establishing relationships of trust, creating open-ended contexts and immers-
ing pupils and students in great writings produces spectacularly successful
language development, and sometimes it doesn't. Many English departments, convinced by the cultural tradition view, drench pupils and students
with literature, then finding their speech as halting, their writing as banal
and their listening and reading as inattentive as ever, turn up the pressure
and provide more of the same. Of course trust, open-ended contexts and
access to writing which can come alive for readers are necessary for full
language growth, but they are not always sufficient. Sometimes pupils and
students also need an informed awareness of what is happening when they
're-use the language' of their culture.

As an example of some of the complexities opened by this debate, we
might consider a piece of writing produced by a group of Year 10 pupils.
The pupils were members of a 'top set' GCSE class in the days before
Dual Certification, and were studying both English Language and English
Literature. Regular lesson time was given over to open access to a well-

stocked library, and most of the pupils read voraciously. The department had a strong literary tradition of the kind referred to by Roger Knight, and the pupils had read and engaged with texts from Shakespeare and Dickens; voluntary reviews of classic novels appeared regularly in pupils' Wider Reading files.

We took seriously Ernst Cassirer's dictum that 'The first language was all in poetry', and placed poetry at the centre of our programme, reading, discussing in groups, preparing dramatized readings and readings with sound effects, acting out, redrafting from alternative points of view, making visual interpretations of (from my records for one half term) Ralph Hodgson's *The Hammers*, Christopher Middleton's *From A Junior School Poetry Book*, Norman Nicholson's *Windscale*, Robert Herrick's *The Hag*, Theodore Roethke's *The Meadow Mouse* and Robert Burns's *To A Mouse*, Wordsworth's *Strange Fits of Passion*, Andrei Voznesensky's *First Ice*, a traditional version of *John Barleycorn*, John Betjeman's *Hunter Trials*, e.e. cummings's *ygUDuh*, Seamus Heaney's *Blackberry Picking* and *Death of a Naturalist* and Adrian Mitchell's *Castaways*. Writing poetry was also given a high priority, and this class too produced its gems; for example these two contrasting visions of the nature of mirth:

Laughter

Down shines the spotlight upon the stage.
The star walks on, a comedian.
The audience applaud on his entrance,
then there is silence
as the audience eagerly await the first joke.

The comedian begins,
first a smirk, then a giggle
ended by guffaws of laughter.
Laughter fills the clubroom,
stomachs feel as though they are going to split.
The noise dies down
as people wipe the tears of laughter away.
What a night!

People Laughing

Curled up into twisting shapes,
Faces curled in roaring laughter,
Twisting and turning as if in pain,
Mouths wide open as dark pits, tonsils showing,
Where from comes laughter of a high pitch.

In the course of a series of lessons on writing plays for radio, one group from this class scripted and recorded the following, *National Hero*:

National Hero: a play for radio

Characters

Kenny: A football supporter
Marlene: Kenny's older sister
Reporter
Football commentator
Radio newsreader

Scene 1   A ward in a French hospital

Reporter: And your sister has travelled by coach from Manchester to visit you?

Marlene: No, it's a place called Heaviley, south of Manchester.

Kenny: No, say Stockport. Brian and Dave will be listening to this.

Reporter: I'll put Heaviley, Stockport for the benefit of our southern readers. Now, your sister tells me this is your first time abroad, Kenny.

Kenny: Yeah. I've always wanted to watch England play in Europe, show them how real football's played.

Reporter: You don't think much of foreign football then?

Kenny: We invented football, didn't we, so we must be better.

Reporter: Does that mean you came to Paris expecting England to beat France?

Marlene: You heard what the nurse said, go easy on him. He was in intensive care all last night.

Reporter: Alright. Kenny, what was your attitude towards the French before the match?

Kenny: We weren't thinking about the French fans. We were just thinking about the game really.

Reporter: Did you consume any alcohol?

Kenny: No – well, not really – a couple of cans of lager.

Reporter: And there was no provocation or animosity?

Kenny: I never said that. I just said we were concentrating on the game. I can't speak for anyone else, just me and the lads.

Reporter: Yet you were stabbed for no apparent reason.

Kenny: But that always happens at these matches. I mean, there's always trouble, that's what Dave and Brian said.

Reporter: So your friends have been involved in football violence?

Marlene: You agreed not to pressure him.

Kenny: It's OK Marl. Listen, they haven't been involved in soccer violence. What I meant was, they've seen it and told me about it.

Reporter: So you decided you'd get your own back and be a national hero?

Marlene: My brother isn't a hooligan you know. He was the victim of an unprovoked attack.

Reporter: A dozen serious injuries, windows smashed and cars burnt out. You should see the state your brother's fellow supporters have left Paris in.

Marlene: Why did you need to interview Kenny if you knew you were going to blame the English fans? I think that's enough for one day. Why don't you just go and write your usual rubbish about thugs disgracing the name of Britain?

Scene 2

Commentator: And with the match in its eightieth minute the French have had most of the play in the second half – the large contingent of English fans have had very little to sing about – until now – yes, Robson is surging forward – shoots – but the shot brings a magnificent save from the French goalkeeper – it's taken upfield – to Dupont – and the English defence is in all sorts of trouble now – Dupont – a left-footed shot – into the top corner – the French fans are going wild – two-nil to France – and some scuffles have broken out – but they seem to be on the French terraces – and it seems to be all over for England this time.

Scene 3

Marlene: Take it easy now Kenny. You'll still be feeling weak for a while.

Kenny: No, I feel alright. It's great to be back home. Can I put the radio on?

Marlene: You haven't even unpacked or had a cup of tea yet. Alright, but at least sit down for a few minutes.

Newsreader: In the wake of last week's football violence in Paris, the French government have announced that a claim against Britain for damage to vehicles and shops will be entered through the European Court of Justice. A British government spokesman refused to comment earlier today, but unofficial sources indicate that measures to prevent British football supporters from travelling abroad are being urgently considered. Now on to financial news.

Kenny: That's bad. I didn't get a mention on that one.

Marlene: What do you mean?

Kenny: Well, I'm somebody now. I was in the papers and on all those news broadcasts.

Marlene: You mean you're proud of it?

Kenny: Why not? It's not every day you get to be famous. I should get some glory for taking on those Frenchies.

Marlene: Are you saying you started all the trouble?

Kenny: Course we did. It was like that reporter said. We went over to get revenge. We can't have foreigners thinking they're better than us, can we?

Marlene: What about those people whose cars your mates smashed up? What about the shops that were looted? Don't you feel anything for those innocent people lying in hospital because of you?

Kenny: What do you mean? I was in hospital myself, remember.

Marlene: You lied to me, you lied to that reporter, to everyone, and now you're whining about your welfare and setting yourself up as a celebrity.

Kenny: Well I am in a way. I must go and see Brian and Dave. City are
               playing that Itie team a week on Saturday, and the lads will be
               expecting their national hero.

National Hero accurately captures the forms of its influences – tabloid
journalism, sports commentary, radio newscasting. Kenny is given a suitably
colloquial voice. The play's structure is skilfully balanced, using the football
commentary as an interscene. Yet despite their advantages, the pupils have
produced a cynical and heartless text. The reporter mouths tabloid clichés in
an unconvincing attempt to chastise Kenny. Marlene challenges the reporter
and then Kenny, but in such a pompous and self-righteous manner that she
is hardly an adequate counterweight to Kenny's casual hypocrisy. The pupils
themselves have learnt no more about football violence, or about the people
involved in it, or about the varieties of language involved than they could
have gained from half-an-hour's informal group discussion.

It is not always possible to predict what preparation will be needed for an
open task, but if the pupils had explored the relationship between language
and values before they had started to write, they might have been less easily
satisfied with stereotypes and clichés. Many of the questions which pupils
could have asked are amenable to their own investigations:

How do words and phrases used by the tabloid press reflect attitudes and
values?
How are conflicts about values worked out within families?
What are the effects of aggressive questioning on the way people express
their views?
What other ways are there to encourage people to explore their opinions and
attitudes?
How do peer groups use language to enhance conformity to their norms?

Some of these questions emerged when the groups in the class shared their
radio plays and commented on them. *National Hero* elicited some praise but
little enthusiasm, and the writers, clearly a little disappointed, asked if it
would be possible for them to try again. We decided first to investigate the
issue of language and peer-group pressure, discussing examples from pupils'
first-hand experience, and reporting on unobtrusively monitored conversations and exchanges in social areas and dinner tables. Forms of address,
particularly nicknames and how their bearers had acquired them, made for
some particularly lively and anecdotal discussion. Pupils noted many individual speech styles: some of their schoolmates talked quickly, or slowly; some
were cheeky; some spoke very confidently, some aggressively, some as if they
were continually apologizing; some had little catch-phrases which were
found either delightful or irritating.

These investigations were not 'exercises' in the linguistic muscle-building
sense of English textbooks, though they were intended as limited and
focused activities related to the dynamics of group interactions and the idiom

of everyday speech in preparation for a wider task. They were informal, took a couple of lessons and involved no written commentary or analysis. My hope was that, at the very least, nobody would place phrases like 'the victim of an unprovoked attack' in the mouths of their characters, though I was aware of the danger that pupils would be tempted into futile attempts at phoney naturalism in their representations of speech. We could have used literary texts, but chose not to, and there is no way of telling whether this would have made any difference. As their second attempt, the group which had written *National Hero* produced the following script, originally called *In the Youth Club*, then retitled *Jo and the Intellectual*:

In the Youth Club *or* Jo and the Intellectual

Characters: Jo, Hughie, Michael, Pippa, Caroline

Scene 1   In the youth club

[A group of boys are on the left, and some girls together on the right]

Hughie: Hey, Mike, fancy a game of pool?
Michael: Ur – no thanks, I just want to sit here and think.
Hughie: Oh, I just want to sit here and think. Come on, just leave him alone.
Pippa: Hey, Jo, I think he's looking at you.
Caroline: Do you think we better leave?
Pippa: No, let's stay and see what happens.
Caroline: I reckon he fancies you, Jo.
Jo: Oh, get lost!
Pippa: No, honestly, I think he does.
Caroline: Jo, you're so lucky! [Sarcastic]
Jo: Oh, come off it you two. I can't help my irresistible charm. I hope he asks me out … [Sarcastic]
Pippa: Shh …. He heard you. He's coming over!
Jo: I don't believe it.
Hughie: Go on, Mike, say your piece!
Michael: Erm – hello.
Jo: Oh, hi.
Michael: Want a drink?
Jo: No, I've got one thanks.
Michael: Oh well, are you doing anything tomorrow night?
Jo: Well, actually, I was, ur, going to Pippa's house.
Pippa: No, it's OK, honestly. It wasn't important. You two go off and enjoy yourselves.
Michael: Oh, I'll meet you outside the cinema at six. [Michael leaves]
Jo: Thanks a lot, Pippa!
Caroline: You're not actually going, are you?
Jo: Oh, yeah, I've fancied him for ages. [Sarcastic]

Scene 2   Outside the cinema

Jo: Hi, sorry I'm late.
Michael: That's OK. The probability of you being early was 59 to 3.

Jo:	Oh, right, well. Where are we going?
Michael:	Well, I was thinking of the Archaeological Museum. It has some fascinating relics about ...
Jo:	Yes, OK, we'll go there then. At least nobody will see me.
Michael:	Pardon? What did you say?
Jo:	Nothing. Let's go.

Scene 3   In the Archaeological Museum

Michael:	... and then Big Hughie fell over the chair leg. [They both laugh]
Jo:	Crickey, is that the time? I said I'd be home for eight.
Michael:	Oh, OK then. Can I see you again?
Jo:	Yeah, sure. What about tomorrow?
Michael:	Confucius says tomorrow never comes, but I'll ring you anyway.
Jo:	OK. Bye.

Scene 4   In the youth club

Hughie:	Hey sis, who's that girl you're going round with?
Pippa:	Who, Caroline?
Hughie:	No, the other one.
Pippa:	Oh, you mean Jo. Why, do you fancy her or something?
Hughie:	I might.
Pippa:	Well hard luck, she's already going out with someone.
Hughie:	Who?
Pippa:	That intellectual, what's-his-name?
Hughie:	You mean Chicken Mike!
Pippa:	Yeah, that's him.
Hughie:	What's she going out with a stupid, boring prat like him for?
Pippa:	Well she obviously doesn't think so.
Hughie:	Oh, I'll have a word with him then.

Scene 5   Outside the cinema

Michael:	Hi!
Jo:	Hi! What's the matter with your eye?
Michael:	Nothing.
Jo:	It looks like something to me.
Michael:	I had a slight mutual disagreement with someone and they damaged my eye tissue.
Jo:	Oh I see. Who was it?
Michael:	I am not in a position to disclose his identity.
Jo:	It was Big Hughie, wasn't it. [Pause] I'll take that as yes.

Scene 6   In the youth club

Jo:	Pippa, did your brother know I was going out with Michael?
Pippa:	Yes, why?
Jo:	What, you told him?
Pippa:	Well, it doesn't matter, does it?
Jo:	No, of course not. Hughie only gave him a black eye.
Pippa:	Well, that wasn't my fault. Anyway, I thought you didn't even want to go with him.

Jo: People can change their minds can't they?
Pippa: Look, Jo, I'm just sick of it. All we hear these days is Michael this and Michael that.
Jo: Well, he's a better friend than you.
Pippa: Thanks a lot. I'll leave you to him then.

This was as far as the group reached with scripting, though they considered several alternative lines for continuation. Michael and Jo lose all their friends, but stay together. They give in to social pressure and split up. Michael retaliates against Hughie and becomes the hero of the hour. Michael turns out to have a sister who is just right for Hughie.

Jo and the Intellectual carries issues, themes and structures over from *National Hero*. The conflict of values between Michael, for peace (he evidently does not strike back against Hughie), honour (he refuses to name his attacker, even to Jo), and the values of the past (his incongruous choice of an archaeological museum for a first date), and Hughie, for violent direct action, echoes Kenny's commitment to national superiority against the civilized outrage of the reporter/sister/government spokesperson. The split between Jo and Pippa over Jo's change of heart echoes the rift which emerges between Kenny and Marlene as Kenny's true colours emerge. Michael's use of language is if anything even more contrived than that of the reporter in *National Hero*, though Hughie's coarseness of temperament is conveyed more economically than Kenny's.

Structurally, *Jo and the Intellectual*, with its abrupt changes of scene, is more scrappy than *National Hero*, though there is an interplay of harmony and discord which offers subtler possibilities for shaping feelings and experiences. From the point of view of language development, however, it is in a different league. Jo's sarcasms – 'I hope he asks me out' and 'I've fancied him for ages' – become retrospective expressions of her real feelings. One stereotype, of Michael as the 'intellectual', is deconstructed, and even Hughie, with his coy 'I might' and his euphemistic 'I'll have a word with him' is given a touch of delicacy. Michael's over-formal language is there to help create a persona, not to convey a public information message. The minor character Pippa, unlike the reporter in *National Hero* who functions as an oral version of an *Express* editorial, acts as plot facilitator by setting Jo up for a date with Michael, then by telling her brother about their relationship. Her language reflects her enjoyment of the conflict and intrigue she has half-created and for which she wants to deny responsibility: 'You two go off and enjoy yourselves', 'Well hard luck', 'Well, that wasn't my fault'.

It might be objected that the issue is not about the kind of learning opportunities which these pupils seized since these are a comparatively minor matter of method; the real battle is for control of curriculum content. It might even be argued that one of the reasons this group of pupils produced *National Hero* was because they were drawing on the jaded and inauthentic language of the media, and that they were able to recover so quickly from their creative bad faith because they had previously built a firm literary base. On this account, literary experience is the essential substrate for language, and particularly writing, development, providing dependable charts for explorations of feeling and thought within experience by giving pupils access to the contextual, historical, connotative possibilities of words. It is interesting to speculate on what directions the group might have taken if instead of following up *National Hero* by investigating language issues they had explored its themes through literary texts.

Nationalism and the triumph of cynicism in *Henry V*? Versions of heroism in *A Tale of Two Cities*? Destructiveness at the heart of experience in *The Sick Rose*? Used unassimilated, such powerful texts simply tempt young writers into parody or plagiarism; fully assimilated, their influence is impossible to isolate. The wind bloweth where it listeth, but in this case exposure to the language of Shakespeare, Dickens and Blake would more likely have proved a tyranny than a release.

Pupils and students may sometimes draw directly on their literary experience for language development. But if a pupil's narrative shares a theme with a Hemingway short story, it is more likely to be because it refers to an important or fundamental aspect of general human experience than because the pupil wants to pay homage to the author. Pupils commonly re-use plots, largely because the cultural stock is finite, but they are as likely to derive them from film, the media, genres from their peer-group cultures such as horror or romance as from the approved canon. How language helps pupils to learn depends more on the transformations enacted on material than on the respectability of their sources. An example can be seen in the following story, again on the theme of relationships between peers and individuals, written by a 14-year-old pupil. At the time it was written, the cinemas were showing a film called *Grease* in which a wistfully virginal girl in an American High School peopled with sexually adventurous students transforms herself into an embodiment of her desired man's fantasy. Another popular film, *The Amityville Horror*, centres on a family who move into a house built on an ancient graveyard.

Wendanitta

One day in the beginning of a new school term, we were all lining up to go into our new classrooms when Mrs McGee our school principal came over with a quaint-looking pretty blonde haired blue-eyed girl.

Principal McGee introduced her to us saying we must look after her and get her used to this school. That would be quite easy with the help of a few certain people. That day when school had finished, Dee, that's me, saw that this new girl with a dress like a convents uniform was very lonely. Me muggins went and asked her what was wrong.

She got talking to me and in the next couple of days we were best of friends. The reason why I said such a thing about her dress was that at Ryndell High the girls don't believe in short mini skirts only pegged pants, black leather jackets, felt skirts, bobby socks and their steady's class ring.

Her name sounded rather queer. It was spelt with a 'wenda', and ended something like 'nittine'.

It was not until she wrote her name all over the cafeteria which was where ours and the gangs were written up.

Her real name was Wendanitta.

One sunny morning when everyone was reading their weekly magazine, Wendy, for short, came dancing into the classroom and sat down and started daydreaming. When Mr Donaldson came strolling into the classroom he sat down and got his file out and told the class what story they were going to do, and immediately saw that Wendy was not paying attention to what he was saying, he got up and shouted at her but she insisted on daydreaming and later when I asked her what she was daydreaming about she said that something was telling her to daydream. Me myself thought that this was a bit strange told two of my girlfriends and they thought I was mad.

One night I heard Wendy talking to herself about being in Omaha where her parents used to live. I gradually caught a few words that night, and then realized that where her parents and her used to live there was a plague that killed all small and large children and where she used to live that's where they were buried in the soil where her house was built. This plague happened about a hundred years ago, and when Wendy went to her old school they taught the children that they shouldn't have anything to do with any children where their buried there. For some stupid idea.

When Wendy and I were alone one evening, she told me all about it when her parents got killed, it was quite a tragic story. Now a couple of years later, Wendy's tombstone is still surrounded with pretty flowers around it, just set back from the school gates.

Wendy's death shocked the whole of Ryndell High because that very day when Principal McGee introduced her to us, she had a way about her that was somewhat very weird.

After that day, she knew she was not going to fit in with all the others. She came to me for sympathy and I surely gave it to her but she killed herself when she knew I had found her secret, with every possible detail to it.

The first three paragraphs of the story, down to 'their steady's class ring' accept the themes of the film *Grease*; peer-group solidarity expressed in modes of dress and romantic involvement; the outsider with old-fashioned values. By tentatively thinking aloud through her writing in order to find a name for her character, the writer is testing Wendanitta's identity for herself. Having the name written 'all over the cafeteria which was where ours and the gangs were written up' signals Wendanitta's desire to belong.

This image starts to subvert the too-easily accepted values of the film, and in the next stage of the narrative the writer codes in parallel images three major areas of her experience to represent in one way or another inner lives and values. She draws on her peer group values for the reference to the girls reading their 'weekly magazines', which expressed their interest in romance and fashion, on her experience of school life for the actions of the teacher, whose file of story titles represents the creativity officially sanctioned by school, and on her memory of the film for 'Wendy came dancing into the classroom and sat down and started daydreaming', introducing the first reference to Wendy's secret experience.

Each image is simple enough on its own, but the juxtaposition produces oppositions and tensions which demand resolution in the narrative. The 'weekly magazines' and the 'teacher's file' signify the values of groups and institutions, while Wendanitta's daydreaming is an assertion of individual consciousness. In another frame of reference, the 'daydreaming' and the 'weekly magazines' are opposed to the values of the school. In trying to reconcile Wendanitta's experience to that of her peer group, the narrator is alienated from her friends, suggesting a fourth image, that of the whole text, *Wendanitta*, as the writer's attempt to resolve for herself the tensions of peer group, school and individual.

In the second half of the story, based loosely on *The Amityville Horror*, larger movements are introduced, distancing the narrative a century, and using the image of the dead children's graves to recapitulate the movement into Wendanitta's loneliness. The writer now controls the emotional effects of her images rather than having them control her; the poignancy of the small distance that separates the lonely person from the group in the picture of Wendanitta's grave 'just set back from the school gates' is a long way from the earlier images of 'bobby socks and their steady's class ring' which foist their stereotypes on the writer.

The narrative process has carried the narrator away from her peer group and into Wendanitta's world, so that 'all the others' no longer fully includes her. Wendanitta's grave takes on a personal significance, becoming to the narrator what the children's graves were to Wendanitta, and representing her discovery that separateness perpetuates itself, just as the narrative that contains this discovery may itself have contributed to the writer's own sense of separateness and individuality.

In spite of this story having been constructed out of genre media products rather than from the great tradition of literature, it contains nothing to imperil that individuality of development so rightly advocated by Dennis Carter. But it does challenge the further step in the argument, that literature, in the sense of 'the accumulated richness of our written inheritance', is the key to the organic growth of language. Works of literature as cultural products have their source in the individual's engagement with the dialectic between language and experience, which is also the living heart of language development. The group who moved from *National Hero* to *Jo and the Intellectual* progressed not in the sense in which the term might be used on a school report, but as we might talk about the progress of a novelist or poet. The writer of *Wendanitta*'s progress is more dramatic because it takes place within a single narrative rather than across two texts, and the stress on the writer's resources takes its stylistic toll, but the process is the same, and it is called literature.

How is a busy English teacher, responsible for as many as 200 pupils each week, spread across eight or nine classes, perhaps on two or three different sites, with the workload of a 100 per cent coursework GCSE, together with pastoral responsibility, administration, curriculum development, possibly even some professional development, to recognize when this process has occurred and when it has not? Reading for assessment is certainly inimical to it. Which of the two radio plays would have received the higher mark for GCSE English? How would you defend *Wendanitta* to your moderator against charges of inappropriate, even ungrammatical, expression, unconvincing overdramatization, lack of originality, poor narrative structure? These pieces would hardly fare much better measured against canonical literary criteria; it is permissible to use the demotic for self-conscious effect (the habit of placing speech marks round terms likely to be identifiable as 'slang' still persists in some classrooms), but teachers schooled in the great tradition might look askance at such lines as 'What's she going out with a stupid, boring prat like him for?' And should we, they might ask, really be including 'Wendy's tombstone is still surrounded with pretty flowers around it, just set back from the school gates' in the same category as 'And many and many a day he thither went/And never lifted up a single stone?'

A linguistic approach means being prepared to take pupils' and students' language use and development seriously, on its own terms, in relation to its own norms. Insofar as it can be described as a language variety, it is not a corrupt or inferior form of adult language, any more than a dialect or creole is a deviant or diminished form of a standard or prestige version of a language. There is abundant evidence to suggest that in the process of acquiring a first language, children are able actively to hypothesize, develop, try out and reformulate theories about language structures and meanings as a matter of routine, and there is no reason to suppose that older pupils and students are any less exploratory and generative. This is not to say that it is enough merely to expose learners to linguistic desiderata to ensure that they learn them, any more than it is sufficient to expose very young children to language without a language acquisition support system, but it does imply that we can trust pupils' and students' own use of language as a secure basis for exploration and development as we create structures and facilitating strategies.

It is standard practice for an English class to use a piece of literature as a starting point or as stimulus material, then to invite pupils or students to pick up the themes. But how often is a piece of student's writing used in this way? If *Wendanitta* was to have such a public as well as a personal, exploratory function, and the discipline of an external audience, it would need redrafting to resolve problems of structure and expression. The components of the final three paragraphs, for example, could be reordered and clarified.

The narrator intervenes directly throughout the story to express her personal view:

quaint-looking
me muggins
The reason why I said ...
Her name sounded rather queer
Me myself thought this was a bit strange
For some stupid idea.
it was quite a tragic story
she had a way about her that was somewhat very weird

A writer who trusted her audience more fully might allow readers to make their own judgements.

Some expressions, perhaps written hastily under pressure from the narrative drive, read oddly or incongruously:

... with the help of a few certain people
It was not until she wrote her name ... (clause remains uncompleted)
she insisted on daydreaming
Me myself thought this was a bit strange told two of my girlfriends
they shouldn't have anything to do with any children where their buried there
she had a way about her that was somewhat very weird

But once these difficulties are resolved, *Wendanitta* suggests several possibilities for investigating aspects of language which would offer some explicit recognition of what the story is struggling to achieve. For example:

• What other films might offer starting points for exploring themes of identity and belonging?
• What values are represented in teenage magazines? How are these expressed in the language they use?
• What images and signifiers for group membership and for individuality are available to us?
• In what circumstances do people keep parts of their lives secret?
• In what circumstances do people confide their secrets to others?

These pupils' texts represent comparatively large learning gains, though most advances in language development are quite unobtrusive, consisting perhaps of an opportunity for a new use of a word, a cadence, a contrast, a shift in narrative perspective. But this fact too holds possibilities. For example, we are familiar with the textbook exercises from which pupils and students toil to correct so-called errors which they are unlikely ever to make. But where are the exercises in which they can comment on, or even simply savour, positive features of their own writing? To redress the balance, here is a model for such a textbook exercise, based on some Year 10 pupil's stories about flying kites and railway journeys:

Appreciate the expression

The following sentences and paragraphs are taken from a set of stories written by a class of Year 10 pupils. Identify what makes them effective, and say what effect each expression has on you:

1 As the wind dropped, his foot caught in the slackened string of the kite.
2 The kite twisted and looped, dived and rose.
3 He watched the wind curl itself round the trees.
4 The broken kite lay limply on the bench.
5 She dragged the kite onto its tail and launched it skyward Harrier-like.
6 My brother took his kite out onto the moors every day after his lunch and before visiting me. I could only lie in bed and watch the striped green and orange kite flying in the sky.
7 She looked round impatiently at the shabby posters of the waiting room.
8 In the distance the lights of the train danced delicately.
9 People in the carriage in front stared out sympathetically, but they did not know how upset I was. Their lives were bright and warm like the train carriages, mine was cold and empty like the desolate station.
10 [A man in a train recognizes one of his former teachers, who is asleep.] I tried to open the sliding door – it stuck fast. My face blushed as everyone turned to watch the idiot wrestle with the door. At last the thing flew to one side with a crash which woke my old teacher with a start.

Or a young writer may find a new measure of control over language. One example is from a Year 9 pupil who, though chatty and witty in social situations, wrote pleasant, well-structured, carefully expressed but rather conventional stories, clearly intended for a teacher-as-examiner audience. About to leave the school to move to another part of the country with her family, she wrote for her classmates a spontaneous account of what she thought she might miss.

I'll miss ...

When I leave I won't miss the big things like our house or the school but the little things like the way the signpost outside our house leans a little bit and doesn't fall in line with the brick. I always meant to straighten it, I must do that sometime before I go.

The patch on my ceiling where my dad fell through from the loft, we never got round to disguising it.

I'll miss things like buying Lisa a cheese butty at lunchtime and lending Alistair my science book when he forgets his. Trying to play badminton with Chloë. And I think I might even miss William's football commentary every Monday. And Tuesday. And Wednesday. And Thursday. And Friday. And ... OK so maybe I won't miss that!

One day maybe I'll yearn for the plonky piano and lurid yellow of the form-room and Andy coming in at lunchtime and adding a little extra unintentional banging at the end of one of my compositions.

Maybe I'll remember fondly Michael telling me how many days, weeks, lessons, minutes, seconds, milliseconds there is until I leave.

Perhaps when I've gone Miss P. will realize that I haven't been to netball practice for the last six weeks. I hope she doesn't realize it in the next week!

I'll miss waiting at the traffic lights for $1\frac{1}{2}$ hours on the way home from school, Mrs S. screaming every time I dye my hair green, and the way that all the clocks in the school show a different time.

I wonder if Lucy will miss the corny jokes. I expect some people will get a couple more detentions when they can no longer copy my homework.

But I wonder if anyone will miss me? I bet everyone'll have forgotten my name after a couple of weeks, but I'll write, promise I will!

No programme of study can legislate for these steps forward, and in the end only the pupils and students themselves can take them. But a linguistic approach which takes the whole language experience of learners seriously can help create conditions to encourage such advances. *I'll Miss ...* draws on resources from the conventions of speech and of writing: 'buying Lisa a cheese butty' and 'OK so maybe I won't miss that' from speech; 'the way the signpost outside our house leans a little bit and doesn't fall in line with the brick' and 'when they can no longer copy my homework' from writing, and their fusion opens up new possibilities of expression. Emboldened, this pupil followed up with a picaresque and hugely enjoyable account of a clairvoyant giraffe's journey by public transport to take part in a cabinet meeting. After she moved she did write to the class as promised, and although her new school was evidently too correct to countenance her new-found writing style, her letters provided a satisfactory alternative forum. This was Dennis Carter's experience in reverse, but with the same respect for principles of trust and the possibilities of open-ended exploration of language experience.

In order to learn, to move forward, learners must necessarily discard parts of what they have learnt. Redrafting, considered so central to writing development by many teachers, is often resisted by pupils and students because of the strong emotional commitment generated by the act of writing. Yet the writers of *National Hero* had to place behind them a text which had cost time and emotional energy. The writer of *Wendanitta* had to move beyond experiences and attitudes which may have helped to define her identity. The writer of *I'll Miss ...* was able imaginatively to move away from a familiar security, in language and real life. In each case a change occurred in the relationship between the finitude of actual text and the network of choices and constraints which constitutes the language system, and at such crucial moments these young writers need teachers with a generous definition of language and an open willingness to encourage its use in accepting and exploring their own feelings, attitudes and relationships.

Language study is already predicated on such a conception. Its premise, that all forms of language are equally complex, systematic and rich, its commitment to speech, its recognition and empirical investigation of the infinite creativity of language, its redefinition of meaning as the relation between signifier and signified rather than word and thing, its respect for the absolute competence of the native speaker, all have important implications for learning which are only now starting to emerge.

Literature enters into this equation not as a store of vicarious experiences to be inherited but rather takes the form of a poetic vision of language and its place in fundamental human experiences. Such a vision is articulated in Andrew Marvell's poem *The Coronet* through the relation between destruction, reconstruction and creativity.

The Coronet

When for the Thorns with which I long, too long,
With many a piercing wound,
My saviours head have crown'd,
I seek with garlands to redress that Wrong:
Through every Garden, every Mead,
I gather flowers (my fruits are only flow'rs)
Dismantling all the fragrant Towers
That once adorned my Shepherdesses head.
And now when I have summ'd up all my store,
Thinking (so I myself deceive)
So rich a chaplet thence to weave
As never yet the king of Glory wore:
Alas I find the Serpent old
That twining in his speckled breast,
About the flow'rs disguis'd does fold,
With wreaths of Fame and Interest.
Ah, foolish Man, that would'st debase with them,
And mortal Glory, Heavens Diadem!
But thou who only could'st the Serpent tame
Either his slipp'ry knots at once untie,
And disentangle all his winding Snare:
Or shatter too with him my curious frame:
And let these wither, so that he may die,
Though set with Skill and chosen out with Care.
That they, while Thou on both their Spoils dost tread,
May crown thy Feet, that could not crown thy head.

The Coronet describes how the poet tries to write a great poem addressed to God, but finding himself desiring praise, asks God either to purify his motives, or to destroy the poem. The main image, of a poem as woven flowers was already a tradition, used for example by Sydney in *Astrophel and Stella:* 'And every flower ... into your poesy wring'. And the coronet, the crown of thorns, the garlands, the fragrant towers, chaplet and curious frame are metamorphosed versions of human actions, including the writing, and the reading, of this poem.

The 'Garden' and 'Mead' of the pastoral tradition are likewise transformed, being appropriated into the Christian tradition with the introduction of the Serpent. A third set of transformations relates to the alternation of creation and destruction; the 'rich ... chaplet' is to be made from the 'fragrant Towers' of love poems; the poem's redeeming humility emerges from the offer of itself as a sacrifice — 'shatter too with him my curious frame'. The reader's attention is drawn back and forth between the poem's two main structural parts by references and parallels which develop the motif of the crown in order to reveal its inadequacy:

Dismantling all the fragrant Towers
Disentangle all his winding Snare

The Thorns with which I ... /My Saviours head have crown'd
Ah, foolish Man, that would'st debase ...

My Saviours head have crown'd
Heavens Diadem

a chaplet
May crown thy Feet

In this way, the interaction between the poem's structure and imagery works the reader towards a resolution of its paradox, that the poem comes into being through a denial of its own validity.

The naive struggles for meaning of *Wendanitta* and *Jo and the Intellectual* may seem a long way from the *The Coronet's* sophisticated paradoxes, but they have in common a willingness to use the creative process to question, subvert and deconstruct their own heuristics, even finally their own presuppositions about cultural values. In each case the possibility of reconstruction depends not on assessment frameworks or nationally prescribed programmes of study, or even the availability of bodies of linguistic knowledge, but on the willingness of individual teachers and classes to develop, monitor, refine, make explicit and if necessary revise, their frameworks for describing to themselves what happens when they use language. In this way it is possible that language experience may find its rightful place at the centre of the English curriculum.

3 Speaking and writing

Education has traditionally promoted literacy, with speech often regarded as a secondary form of language. Academic linguistics, by contrast, has concentrated mainly on spoken forms, with phonetics and phonology accorded very high priority as bases for describing language forms. In recent years, teachers' growing awareness of the importance of oracy in learning, and a growing realization by linguists that writing has its own norms and rationale has helped to move the two positions closer together. Since many misapprehensions about language can be traced to confusions about the relation between speaking and writing, it is not surprising that teachers and linguists have been able to cooperate on this subject with the aim of facilitating pupils' and students' movement between the two modes. Interactional approaches, which focus on discourse rather than texts, process rather than product, dynamic systems rather than static structures, have been particularly valuable since they emphasize the roles of speakers and hearers, readers and writers in the processes, many of them social and psychological as well as linguistic, which generate the meanings conveyed through spoken and written texts.

An interactional approach to speech can be illustrated by an exchange between three Year 7 pupils, taken from a small-group discussion on the theme of winter. In some ways these three pupils, Matthew, Daniel and Catherine, made an ideal discussion group. Matthew was ebullient and outspoken. Catherine, no less forceful, was more thoughtful, often ready with a challenging question in response to conventional views. Daniel, a natural arbiter, was happy to listen constructively and to intervene at key points in order to summarize, balance and integrate other people's views. An extract from this discussion is as follows:

Extract from a discussion between three Year 7 pupils

Matthew: I go sledging
Daniel: I do

Catherine: I haven't got a sledge but I go
Daniel: I do
Catherine: on plastic bags sometimes
Matthew: we might get a sledge next week
Daniel: well I've got my sledge this year
Matthew: my cat – well – ur – my – me and my sister – 's cat – um – loves playing in the snow
Catherine: my cat – my cat is just the opposite – well
Matthew: when I was ten – we've got this sort of ledge in our bedroom and my brother pulled open the window and got out onto the ledge – he got a snowball and he said do you dare me to do it – so he threw it and it splattered all over my bed
Catherine: where I used to live before it was – it was snowing a lot – and this – this id – I think – man – he was a bit thick I should think because he was – he was shovelling all the snow on the road and making it even worse for the cars

The skirmishes about who does and who doesn't have a sledge, and Catherine's pointed reply to Matthew that 'my cat is just the opposite' alert us to the underlying conflict between these two pupils. They also help us to make sense of Catherine's difficulties in composing her anecdote about the man shovelling snow onto the road. Catherine's account mirrors Matthew's in structure, and seems to be a veiled criticism of what she may perceive as thoughtless silliness. On the face of it, Catherine has simply been reminded by Matthew's story of an event from her childhood. But her story also includes a judgement, seemingly on the man shovelling snow, but also perhaps, by implication, on Matthew and his brother. Catherine has made her point to her own satisfaction; Matthew may or may not have picked up the suggestion that 'someone who makes things worse must be a bit thick'. In any case, the discussion moved on to other matters.

One problem with the differences between speech and writing approach to such ephemeral exchanges is that its focus is inevitably on surface features such as pauses, hesitations, loops, interpolations, rewordings. If Catherine had written her account, it might have read as follows:

> I remember an incident which happened where I used to live before I moved here. It was snowing heavily and a man was shovelling snow onto the road making it more dangerous for the cars which came past. I don't think it was a very sensible thing to do.

The written version edits out Catherine's hesitation over how to characterize the man ('this id ... – [idiot?] – I think – man'), alters 'even worse' to 'more dangerous', making it more difficult to generalize the implied judgement to other situations, and replaces the personal judgement 'a bit thick' with a more cautious general criticism. It may be instructive for pupils and students to consider these changes, though the point of the exchange only emerges in its interactional context, and then only briefly and subtly.

However, the widespread and deeply-rooted effects of emphasizing writing to the detriment of speech can be seen in many pupils' and students' ideas about the relation between speaking and writing. These conceptions emerge in such statements as:

We do not speak in sentences.
Spoken language contains many deviations from Standard English.
The omission of letters to shorten words is common in speech.
Spoken language tends to contain more grammatical mistakes than writing.
Spoken English is unstructured.

These statements were all written by 16+ A Level English Language students near the start of their courses, and probably reflect the social consensus rather than the views of the teachers. Whatever the source, pupils and students have a right to some defences against such misapprehensions. Prejudice is not best countered by antithetical prejudice, and the only other possibility is principled observation. One approach might be to ask whether actual utterances verify or disprove explicit statements about speech. In this case we might ask whether the following transcript of an extract from an impromptu talk given by a 15-year-old pupil as part of his GCSE Oral Assessment supports these general evaluations.

A winter morning

right well I woke up at six but – I looked out the window and the snow was everywhere and I thought – it's going to be cold – I went back to bed and I got up about half six – yeah – I put my gloves on – that's my sheepskin gloves – well warm – and it was freezing – it was just freezing – I started my paper round at seven and finished it half past and oh it was freezing ah yeah I met this bloke who was – he was like – you know that one he – on the market you know – he spends his money on um – cider – he was walking down the road and he – he was on about 1962 or something – it was up to my windows and all that – I left our house at eight o'clock and oh it was freezing – I walked to school and it was well cold – the snow was blowing on my face and everything and – little brats were lobbing snowballs and that at everyone – chucking them – at people – anything – cars and – if I get my hands on them I'll kill them – I was dead warm – it was cold on my face like but – I was dead warm – three miles I walked this morning or it could have been four miles

The suggestion that 'we do not speak in sentences', though partly borne out by this transcript, obscures more interesting features related to discontinuities occasioned by narrative planning in speech. For example, at the start of the account, the speaker presumably intends to say 'I woke up at six but I got up at half six', but as he utters the first clause, decides to interpolate details of what happened between these two events. A similar structure occurs with the account of the man talking about the winter of 1962; we might speculate that the initial sentence at the planning stage may have been 'I met this bloke who was on about 1962 or something' (or 'who was walking down the street'), but that as the first clause was being uttered, the speaker realized the need to identify the character more fully for his audience, and inserted the information about the man's association with the market and his drinking habits before completing that second clause which constituted the main point for the theme of the narrative, winter.

The anecdote does contain some non-standard forms. In particular, we might identify these words and phrases:

well warm well cold
I looked out the window
I finished it half past
this bloke
he was on about 1962
little brats
lobbing
chucking
dead warm

Only two of these items, 'I looked out the window' and 'I finished it half past' are non-standard in the sense of belonging to a regional dialect form. 'Well' as an adjective intensifier identifies the speaker as belonging to a particular age group, and is non-standard in the sense that the usage is currently limited to this group. 'Dead' + 'adjective' has never gained respectability despite common use over several decades, and older speakers tend to avoid using it. 'Bloke' and 'chucking' have long been used as colloquial synonyms for 'man' and 'throwing', as has 'lobbing,' which also has a technical meaning. 'To be on about' something is used throughout the speech community to suggest a degree of listener incomprehension. 'Brat' is hardly even colloquial, having wide currency and clear pejorative connotations.

The general validity of the claim that spontaneous speech deviates markedly from Standard English depends on how this term is characterized. If it is defined as having the lexical and grammatical features normally associated with unmarked formal written English, then speech is certainly quite different in character from it, and all the selected items from the pupil's anecdote would count as non-standard. But if it is defined more broadly as the variety or dialect normally used by middle-class speakers in most parts of the UK, then the only convincing examples of non-standard English would be 'I looked out the window' and 'I finished it half past'.

The idea that 'the omission of letters to shorten words is common in speech' is just nonsense on the face of it, since spoken words do not consist of letters but of phonemes, or speech sounds. However, amending *letters* to *phonemes* does not necessarily rescue the suggestion because the idea of omission only makes sense if there is assumed to be a 'standard' or paradigm form of a word, from which all other pronunciations are deviations. In connected speech, the 'sound-shape' of a word constantly alters according to its context, and we have to redefine our idea of a 'word' to allow for its protean character. For example, the 'shortened words' suggestion might put forward these examples from the pupil's account of his winter morning:

an I thought   (/d/ is omitted in 'and')
he spenz iz money   (/d/ is omitted in 'spends', and /h/ in 'his')

The conventional, and unverifiable, judgement on these pronunciations is that they are 'sloppy'. If this is so, then other normal pronunciation processes including such assimilations as 'I wemp back to bed, ik could have been', which confer a sense of ease and fluency on speech, would have to be characterized in the same way.

In spite of the fact that, from a descriptive point of view, the grammar of a language system is a construct out of the actual utterances of speakers, the view that *spoken language tends to contain more grammatical mistakes than writing* is surprisingly widespread. It may be that the relevant feature here is not grammaticality but tidiness. A written version of the pupil's anecdote would certainly have edited out switches in direction, interpolations and interaction markers, so that the incident in which he meets the man from the market might read like this:

> I met this bloke from on the market, the one who spends his money on cider.
> He was walking down the road and he was on about 1962 or something. 'It was up to my windows,' and all that.

An utterance such as 'He – he was on about 1962' is not as neat as 'He was on about 1962', but it is not ungrammatical in the way that 'He 1962 was on about' fails to conform to the normal English order of subject–verb–object.

To claim that *spoken English is unstructured* suggests that the elements of spoken texts can occur in random order. The pupil's account contains a chronological line expressed in clearly differentiated episodes, and the loops and interpolations indicate attempts to find appropriate points to include background information and personal reaction by the narrator. The structure is determined by a number of factors, including the narrator's choice of focus on key events and aspects and his awareness of his audience, compounded by the need to monitor several events at different levels of description simultaneously. No doubt the narrative elements would have been more carefully integrated in a written account, but the view that speech is *un*-structured preempts some interesting questions about how speakers actually manage to organize events, characters, responses, background information, transitions from one episode to the next, into a text with enough coherence to be understood by a listener.

What this analysis shows above all is that the proper starting point for exploring the nature of spoken language is spoken language itself used as evidence to test out pupils' and students' own ideas. In this respect, the *Cox Report*, normally so careful to avoid hidden agendas, sets up potentially misleading parameters for this area of language study by insisting that pupils examine the *differences* between spoken and written language. The National Curriculum for English requires that pupils should be able to:

Level 6   Demonstrate, through discussion and ... writing, grammatical differences between spoken and written English.

Level 8   Demonstrate knowledge of organizational differences between spoken and written English.

Some of the problems in the approach suggested by these statements of attainment emerged in one of my own early attempts to explore this issue with a class of Year 9 pupils. The initiative predated the national curriculum, and emerged from an attempt to explore with younger pupils some of the ideas which had been raised in work with groups of 16+ students on A Level English courses, but the principles are the same.

My aim was to give my Year 9 mixed-ability class an opportunity to explore some language differences between spoken and written accounts using a set of drawings of people in various situations. The pupils worked in pairs to describe what was happening from the point of view of a person in the picture, and each account was recorded. There was a strong sense of, 'Why are we doing this?' from the class, perhaps because I had failed to place the exercise in a context to which the pupils could relate. Most pupils offered a minimum requirement response, and those who gave more limited themselves to fairly literal descriptions and banalities. Typical examples, transcribed, were as follows:

Spoken account based on a picture of a girl holding a ladder, with a van in the background

um me – me and my friend have just ur started a business and – um – window cleaning – and we've got a van – with our name on – on it and um – what we do and what number to ring – and you – if you want your windows cleaning – and um – it's a totally boring job – and – but at least it was a nice day for the first day

Spoken account based on a picture of three people in an outdoor market, two of them making aggressive gestures at each other, the third trying to intervene

I've just come down to the market with my friend – ur – Sid – we can do the stall um – I went off to get a cup of coffee and I've come back and he's having a go at the old man – because he's ur tried to take some things from our stall – I had to stop him but the stall's all wrecked so we had to go home

I duplicated copies of the transcripts and gave them to the class the next lesson. The transcripts caused some consternation among the pupils, unused as they were to seeing speech written down so directly, and particularly as it was their own. We listened to the tape again to confirm that the transcripts really did represent what had been said, pauses, 'um's and 'ur's and all.

I then asked each pair to turn its transcript into a written account, hoping that this would offer material for exploring differences between speaking and writing. Most of the pupils simply edited out the fillers and formalized the syntax. One or two developed their material in tentatively narrative directions. The most promising was the account of the people at the market stall:

Written version of the spoken account based on a picture of three people in an outdoor market

Me and Sid have a stall on the market. We sell cushions, curtains and carpets. The market is every Saturday and Wednesday. Today is Saturday. We went down at 7 a.m. and started to set the stall up. A pair of curtains were a bit ripped so we put them at the back.

By this time my back was aching, so we popped off for a cup of coffee. Sid went back then to look after the stall. Suddenly he cried, 'Jim! Come quick!' The stall was wrecked. Sid started hitting an old man, so I had to stop him and the old man ran off. We couldn't do the stall that day.

When the pupils turned to discuss the differences between the spoken and the written accounts, they observed that the written versions tended to be longer, used full stops and had more things happening, but the motivation to analyse in detail was noticeably lacking. Judging that this activity had reached the end of its usefulness for the time being, I laid it aside.

A further attempt with an older, Year 10, class later in the year was more successful. This time the focus was on spoken accounts as preparation for narrative writing for GCSE assessment, and pupils were given more control over how they worked in terms of groups and use of cassette recorders. However, the pattern of 'talk and record', 'transcribe', 'redraft', 'discuss' remained the same, and this time the difficulties of using comparison as a way of exploring the nature of speech emerged more clearly.

Of the anecdotal accounts which emerged from this project, my own favourite as a possible basis for writing was a story about the long summer days of childhood which contained interesting themes about the experience of time. As it happened, though the pupil recognized the account's possibilities, she chose to retain the simplicity of the original and in her formal written version did little more than trim the pauses and repetitions. Her transcribed account is as follows:

Spoken account of an incident from early childhood

I used to live up near the fire station – you can cut across the back fields to get into Dog Wood – and we went – we were in there and we used to spend abs – absolutely all day every day there – um – in the holiday – we used to get really dirty and everything – and ur – this was about five years ago now I suppose – and we were – we were up there – and ur – the time went really quickly – and it was in the summer so you don't really think about it – and none – none of us had brought a watch with us and um – we were there till about six o'clock – but we weren't sure what time it was and we'd told our parents we'd be back at six – and Emma reckoned she could read – tell the time by the sun – but we all believed her – she was there saying – you know it's only about four o'clock – looking at the sun – you know – moving round the trees – so – we decided – and eventually – I don't know what time it must have been but it was summer so it was still light – it was about half past ten at night and all our parents came walking through the wood with all the dogs and everything – and we were still there playing when they found us

One account by a pupil of a recent experience was altered considerably in its transformation into a written narrative. The transcript is followed immediately here by the pupil's own formal written version:

Spoken account of buying a present for a wedding anniversary

what happened was it was my parents' wedding anniversary and I wanted to buy them a teapot – so – we couldn't get one in town so we planned to go into Manchester – so I bought this teapot – and ur – I dropped it and smashed it in the street – right – so – when we got back I didn't have anything for my parents' wedding anniversary – so – I was talking to Ann at the door – and mum was listening – and she walked in and she had this mass epi [a severe and angry telling off] and said you've been to Manchester and she rang her parents and now we can't do anything or go anywhere without our parents ringing each other to check

Written account of buying a present for a wedding anniversary

An Anniversary Present

I wanted to buy something as a present for my parents for their fifteenth wedding anniversary, and I'd remembered my mum saying she needed a new teapot. I went all round town but I couldn't find one I liked, so I asked my friend Ann if she'd come to Manchester with me to buy one. We couldn't say anything because it was meant to be a surprise. We went on the train, and walked round all the shops until I saw this one I liked. It was blue with an old-fashioned spout and handle for £10.99. I bought it, but by that time it was late so we had to run for the train, and I fell over and dropped the teapot. It smashed into bits all over the pavement. I just wanted to cry, but Ann said don't worry, we'll find something else.

When we got home I was still upset, and I was just talking to Ann about it on our doorstep when mum opened the door. She'd heard everything. She was so angry we'd been into Manchester without permission, and of course I couldn't explain why we'd been. She rang up Ann's parents, and they grounded her for a week. Now they ring each other up every time either of us goes out of the house.

Using this pair of transcript/written account, together with some others, produced some genuine explorations from the pupils. They observed, among other things, that the written account:

was longer
had a title
gave a more important role to the writer's friend Ann

contained more details, for example in describing the teapot and giving the
price, which may have been intended to help the reader to feel something
of the writer's loss

explained more about why people did certain things, for example why the
writer chose to buy a teapot, why she didn't tell her parents she was going
to the big city, and why the writer's mother was angry

didn't use slang, for example in writing, 'She was so angry ...' rather than,
'She had this mass epi ...', though there was some disagreement about
whether 'grounded' counted as slang or not

'flowed better', was 'easier to understand' and 'helped you to picture what
was happening'

Most of these suggestions were developed more or less unprompted by the
pupils working in groups, and they had clearly learnt something about the
relationships between a written and a spoken text. However, my next objective was to try to find ways of exploring some of the grammatical similarities
and differences, and since I judged that this perspective would be more likely
to frustrate than to motivate this Year 10 class, I took the accounts to a class
of 16+ A Level English Language students, who were accustomed to analysing the language of texts. The comments which follow represent what I
learnt in the process of working with this class to try to describe some of the
grammatical similarities and differences between the spoken and the written
versions of *An Anniversary Present*. We found that grammatical differences
alone are very hard to pin down out of the context of content, vocabulary
and textual organization. For example, on what terms can the following be
compared?

1 Spoken text: I wanted to buy them a teapot
2 Written text: I wanted to buy ... a present ... and I'd remembered my
   mum saying she needed a new teapot

(1) is a direct statement, and (2) more indirect, following the process of the
writer's decision in its stages. Taken as a whole, (2) is more complicated,
with its conjunction of two sentences, and more complex, with its embedded
participial clause, 'my mum saying ...', but the comparison is not really fair
because the two statements are quite different functionally. If we compare
only those components which are conveying the same or similar information,
there is little difference in complexity:

1 Spoken text: I wanted to buy them a teapot
2 Written text: I wanted to buy ... a present

When we did find two sentences which seemed more obviously comparable,
the differences turned out to be of little significance:

3 Spoken text: It was my parents' wedding anniversary and I wanted to buy
   them a teapot

4 Written text: I wanted to buy something as a present for my parents for their fifteenth wedding anniversary

We noted the expansion of 'my parents' wedding anniversary' to 'their fifteenth wedding anniversary', and the reordering of elements which transforms an indirect object pronoun into an adverbial which contains a more explicit noun phrase:

3 Spoken text: I wanted to buy them a teapot
4 Written text: I wanted to buy something ... for my parents

Other comparisons found us unable to separate grammatical differences from differences in content. For example:

5 Spoken text: we couldn't get one in town ...
6 Written text: I went all round town but I couldn't find one I liked

(6) does contain additional detail in 'all round town', indicating the effort the writer made, and 'couldn't find one I liked', indicating the writer's determination to find something more than a token present. But these could hardly be described as grammatical differences, even though the differences in implied motivation and writer's attitude are expressed through different grammatical patterns.

It occurred to us that in order to capture variations between grammar in speech and grammar in writing, we might need to go to a higher level of generality, and one suggestion from the students was that speech grammar is in some ways simpler than written grammar. This attractive suggestion proved very difficult to test. The idea that complexity could be assessed by counting words per sentence was tried, but soon discounted because of the difficulty of what counts as a sentence. A sentence is easy to identify in writing by means of punctuation, but what is a sentence in speech? Should conjunctions such as 'and' and 'so' count as sentence boundary markers, like full stops in writing, in which case the spoken text could be said to contain many simple sentences? Or should the conjoined clauses all count as one super-sentence, which would have the effect of greatly increasing the 'complexity' of the spoken text on this criterion? Using words per clause as an alternative proved impracticable because of lack of comparability; for example the content of some clauses in the spoken text was expressed as noun phrases in the written text, e.g.:

7 Spoken text: It was my parents' wedding anniversary ...
8 Written text: their ... wedding anniversary

Another suggestion, that writing contains more subordinate clauses than speech, was tested, but proved inconclusive. The most complex sentence in the written text was:

| I'd remembered | my mum saying | she needed a new teapot |
| Clause 1 | Clause 2 | Clause 3 |

Clause 1 contains Clause 2, which itself contains Clause 3. But this statement would not have been out of place in a spoken account. And in any case, the final sentence of the spoken account clearly rivals it, as an informal clause analysis shows:

we can't do anything|or go anywhere|without our parents ringing each other|to check
Clause 1   Clause 2   Clause 3   Clause 4

Clauses 3 and 4 taken together are 'subordinated to' Clauses 1 and 2 taken together. What this difficult, and often frustrating, investigation showed to us was that comment on grammar cannot be separated from comment on other aspects of the expression of textual meaning and content. In particular, the relation between grammar and textual organization was very close. The type and variety of grammatical structures used was related to explanations, background details and expansions of the narrative. The place of the narrator in each text also influenced the grammar, since the written text contained a richer narrator presence, and an attendant richness of 'psychological' verbs, such as 'want', 'remember', 'like', giving added weight to the reader's interpretation of the narrator's motivations and also adding potential complexity to the grammar, since these verbs tend to collocate with a variety of complex structures, such as catenatives ('I wanted to buy ...'), participial clauses ('I'd remembered my mum saying ...') and relative clauses ('... find one I liked).

This experience does not augur well for the National English Curriculum's requirement at Level 6 that pupils 'Demonstrate, through discussion and ... writing, grammatical differences between spoken and written English', but suggests that the more fruitful strategy might be to focus on the Level 8 requirement that pupils 'Demonstrate knowledge of *organizational* differences between spoken and written English' and try to include Level 6 in that discussion.

An interactional model of the relation between speaking and writing can help us to judge the appropriate use of each mode for achieving specific aims. For example, certain kinds of tentative exploration are best effected through the interactional functions of speech, whereas some forms of equally exploratory but more focused kinds of thinking can only be achieved by means of the structural disciplines more normally associated with writing. Enforcing an inappropriate combination of the two modes can lay a dead hand on possibilities for language development, as the following example illustrates. As part of a series of lessons for Personal and Social Education I had given a group of Year 8 pupils a short newspaper report about a girl who had started to behave uncharacteristically badly at school.

Screams from girl in court

A girl was carried screaming from the court today when she was remanded to prison.

The girl, aged sixteen, was charged with causing wilful damage to fittings at school.

The deputy headteacher of the school said the girl was too unruly and posed a danger to other pupils. 'There has been particular difficulty with her since 21 May,' she said.

When the magistrates announced that she would be remanded to prison, the girl began struggling and kicking. She was heard to shout, 'Why should I go to prison? I'm not bad.'

The pupils were to discuss some of the possible reasons why this had happened in preparation for a roleplay to explore the idea of behaviour in school. On this occasion, I asked one member of the group to write down the ideas which emerged from the discussion. After some time spent talking about who should act as secretary, the pupils' discussion went as follows:

Laura: now listen listen – we have to ask questions
Keri: why did the girl – why did the girl – um – go bad
Laura: maybe – it was because of problems at home – maybe
Keri: not – not necessarily – she could have – it could have been natural
Alice: I don't think it
Laura: it could have been – it could have been ur
Keri: I think her mum and dad must have divorced ur – or something like that – I think or
Alice: or her mum wanted – her mum might have beaten her up
Laura: or maybe she went mad
Alice: write it down – write it down – write it down
Laura: twenty-first of May – causes
Alice: causes of
Laura: causes of disruptance – twenty-first of May
Keri: causes of – divorce
Alice: at home
Keri: or beaten up
Laura: problems at home I'll just put
Keri: or
Alice: problems at home
Laura: or maybe she wasn't as good as the – ur – other children at school
Keri: problems at home
Nerys: problems in the family
Keri: problems at home is problems in the family – anyway – um
Laura: let's see why she didn't – um –
Keri: covers almost everything – problems at home problems at school – it covers almost everything doesn't it
Laura: not necessarily – no what I mean is what I mean is
Nerys: go on – carry on
Alice: we're all listening
Laura: no no – listen – as secretary – I've got to – ask questions
Keri: you haven't – you've only got to write them down
Alice: oh listen – come on – what about
Laura: she could – she – it might be true actually – well it could all be true
[Discussion collapses for several minutes.]

The discussion begins with promising 'maybe's, 'could have's, 'or's and 'might have's, only to stiffen into formulae as the secretary is reminded of her duty to write ideas down, so that her attempt to revive exploration of possibilities is overruled by the group's consensus that she is acting beyond her responsibilities.

As this example, and daily classroom experience confirms, there is more to the relationship between speaking and writing than grammar and textual organization. They are certainly not the only factors which pupils and students have to contend with, and if teachers focus entirely on these aspects they would be likely to distort the very complex, but implicit, model of the speech–writing relationship which a learner adopts as a framework to facilitate the movement between one mode and the other. The principle of developing what is already present within a learner's heuristic by adjusting such controllable task parameters as speaker/writer role, purpose and audience is more likely to be successful than making vain attempts to manipulate the details of a learner's grammatical and organizational mechanisms.

For example, the following transcript of an anecdote from a Year 9 pupil bears all the hallmarks of casual spoken narrative addressed to peers with whom the speaker shares terms of reference.

> down at the industrial estate – a few years ago – on this building site and me and Malc were there – we were just playing in a building site – playing ticky and everything – there were – drainpipes and everything – we were doing like Scottish people do – going like that – and chucking them – and – there was this dumper – ur – with six-inch nails in it – we got Len Harrington on this wall and started throwing nails at it like at the – knife-throwing – and then he got in this dumper and he took the handbrake off and he said he said come on this and he pushed me in and it knocked the wall down – on this building site and the police got us – and they charged us with – the damage – but we were let off

The speaker shares knowledge of people and places with his listeners. He assumes common experience of games and the general contents of a building site with 'playing ticky and everything' and 'drainpipes and everything'. The use of 'the' throughout in preference to 'a' may indicate that the speaker is using language to help himself visualize the scene and therefore to prompt his own memory of the events. He appeals to a wider commonality of experience with his references to tossing the caber, supported by mimetic actions 'like this,' and to circus knife-throwers. In terms of values, 'just playing' and 'he pushed me in and it knocked the wall down' suggest that the speaker wants it understood that he is not to be considered at fault for the mishap.

A further staging point in the transition from the spoken to the written form may be represented by the following account written by another Year 9 pupil, as part of a module of lessons devoted to pupils writing their own autobiographies, which shows clear evidence of an emerging writing style, but a lack of control over conventions of written English.

My beginning

When I was born my mother already had one child called Paul and as I grew up I used to have fights with him. When I was about 11½ months old I started walking I can't remember anything else apart from when I was about 3½ I had one of those bikes that you pushed with your feet and I was at my nans when this happened, so, I was going around this corner and I fell off and hit my face on the floor and swallowed my 2 front teeth. So my mum and dad rushed me to hospital and on the day they let me out I sat on the bed but fell off and broke my rib. And I remember when I was about 10 and I was on the building site and we used to have mud bomb fights that's where you throw stones at each other anyway as I threw this stone all these bricks fell on my hand and nearly chopped my thumb off and my mate Ric James was with me and I said to him 'ugh' look at my thumb and he was nearly sick then I stared at it and started crying and ran home but you had to climb over this fence and I couldn't get over so I had to get on Ric's back to get over it. Well when I got home I told my mum I had fallen off my bike because I was scared of getting done. And I've still got the scar today.

It would be oversimple to claim that Michael writes as he speaks, though this text has much in common with a spoken account. The planning is mainly short-range, with one incident stimulating the memory of another. Michael's interposing of information as it occurs to him is one clear example of his response to the organizational challenge of ordering background details, explanations and narrative. For example, the placing of the italicized elements in the following extracts would be perfectly natural in speech, as transcripts quoted earlier in this chapter show, but in a written account they are checks on the reader's ability to follow the narrative line.

> when I was about 3½ I had one of those bikes that you pushed with your feet and *I was at my nans when this happened*, so, I was going around this corner

> I was on the building site and we used to have mud bomb fights *that's where you throw stones at each other* anyway as I threw this stone all these bricks fell on my hand

Michael's use of conjunctions to mark clause and sentence boundaries, his inclusion of such interaction markers as 'anyway … well', and his choice of such words and phrases as 'one of those bikes', 'nans', impersonal 'you', 'my mate', 'Ric', 'getting done', as well as use of 'this' and 'these' for indefinite reference, all serve to help create a sense of written-down speech. One clear indication that Michael is processing his account in the spoken rather than the written mode is his first sentence:

> When I was born my mother already had one child called Paul

In spoken English, 'called Paul' would be uttered as a separate tone group, but as Michael has written the sentence it also has an incongruous non-restrictive interpretation.

However, it is important to recognize that Michael does have control over some important aspects of the written mode, including some significant grammatical constructions. The intended scope of the account, from 'When I was born' to 'still ... today', is on a more ambitious scale than might normally be associated with spoken anecdotes. The use of ellipsis in 'I sat on the bed but fell off' is more characteristic of writing than speech. The penultimate sentence, 'when I got home I told my mum I had fallen off my bike because I was scared of getting done', with its complex embedding of coordination and subordination, is evidence that Michael is planning in units greater than a single clause.

Intervention to extend these skills might take several forms. The most direct, and probably the least effective, would be to encourage Michael to practise constructions through drills and exercises. These normally have the negative aim of correcting unwanted patterns, and their scope is usually limited to easily identifiable structures, such as 'When I was born my mother already had one child, called Paul.' The greater part of what a learner needs to move between spoken and written modes – narrative organization, clause planning, decisions about whether to mark a clause or sentence boundary with a conjunction or a full stop, use of lexis to indicate the level of formality of a text – are too subtle or diffuse to be accessible to this gross approach.

A more promising strategy would be to ensure that the scheme of work for Michael's language development includes opportunities for him to engage in tasks which are likely to require the characteristic features of formal written language, while at the same time allowing him to use his characteristic spoken 'voice' as a resource. Supported by a framework of diverse experience in reading and listening, and by more explicit discussion of language issues, including those related to similarities and differences between speaking and writing, with a clear role for Michael as a writer and the discipline of a well-defined intended reader, this approach is more likely to allow Michael to draw on his language experience in order to develop an appropriate structure and style.

Such a scheme need not be highly programmatic. It might simply take the form of a series of opportunities for pupils and students to explore themes close to their own concerns and language experience within a framework of open discussion about how speech and writing relate to each other. The movement between speech and writing is certainly not all one way and a teaching and learning model which denies pupils access to the vast resources of their own speech is likely to limit and stultify their writing development as well as conveying negative messages about the nature of spoken language. Facilitating language development means helping learners to stay in touch with all aspects of their language experience so that they can select and deploy them when the moment is right. The scale of this task is illustrated by the two stories which follow. Both were written by a pupil called Jill, the first when she was 12 years old, the second when she was 16.

The mystery of the castle

We were on our way to Cornwall by eleven o'clock. I was taking with me my friend Lucy. We stopped a few times to have something to eat and drink. By four o'clock we were outside the large oak door, with studs along each side. We dragged the heavy suitcases out of the car boot and up the stone steps.

We walked into the castle; it had been made into an hotel. My Dad signed in at the desk, and the lady behind it rang a bell and a man dressed in a black suit came into the room. The lady told him to show us to our rooms. He picked up two of our cases, which happened to be the smallest and lightest. He started to walk up the stairs, and we followed dragging the suitcases with us. At last, we came to our room, we were exhausted after we had walked up about a thousand steps. The butler was not at all tired, but he had the smallest cases. He stood near the door for a minute or two, as if he was waiting for a tip. He scowled, as my dad told him that we wouldn't need him any more. He left slamming the door behind him. I decided I didn't like him.

Lucy and I had a separate room from my mum and dad. As we lay in our beds, I thought I heard a noise, but as it didn't come again I soon fell asleep. I was awoken in the middle of the night by Lucy shouting my name. 'What is it?' I asked and then I heard what she had heard. A low moaning sound followed by a sharp tapping was circling round and round our room. We were terrified. After about ten minutes the noise stopped. We talked about it for a while and decided not to wake my mum and dad up. We eventually fell asleep.

The next morning while we were having breakfast we told my mum and dad what had happened. They told the manager and he said that complaints had been made before about it, and we could change rooms if we wished. We said we would stay because they probably wouldn't come again. That afternoon we were in the big lounge watching a film show when suddenly about four men charged into the room with guns. I recognised one of them as the butler that had carried our cases. They told us all to sit down, or someone would be shot. Everyone did as they were told. Then they began to tie people up. I was frightened, but I thought of a plan. I started to moan loudly. 'Be quiet,' a man shouted. 'I feel awful, I think I am going to be sick,' I moaned, holding my sides. I made a funny noise as though I was about to be sick. One of the men said, 'Let her go to the bathroom. She can't do anything, she's only a kid.' I walked out of the room still moaning. As soon as I was out of sight, I ran to the nearest telephone. 'Only a kid,' I thought. 'I'll show them.' I rang the police and told them what had happened. Then I hid myself in a wardrobe and locked it from the inside. About ten minutes later I heard a man's voice, 'Where is the wretched child?' I hid behind some coats inside the wardrobe. He tried the door of the wardrobe, but finding it locked went away again.

A little while after that I heard a police siren and I unlocked the wardrobe and rushed to the window. The police were knocking the door down. I ran to the top of the stairway and I could see the police fighting the men. As there were more policemen than gun men they soon had handcuffs on and were pushed into the lounge. It was there they confessed everything. From what I understood, a man had offered them a large sum of money for the hotel and estate, so they were trying to take over. They were also trying to scare people away with strange noises. The police drove off with the gunmen and I never saw them again.

The source of *The Mystery of the Castle* is clearly the Enid Blyton adventure story, though Jill transforms the castle into an hotel to bring the setting a little closer to her own possible experience. The scope of the narrative is wide, but the action is arbitrary and characters other than the narrator are sketchy and motiveless. The narrator's disproportionate desire to punish the hotel porter with prison for not carrying the family's heavy suitcases looks particularly unhealthy.

Yet beyond the Famous Five clichés of studded oak doors, endless staircases, low moaning sounds and mass kidnaps, there may be a reading of this story which offers some possibilities for language development. The narrator exercises initiative to establish control over powerful adults while at the same time retaining a sense of security. Having locked herself into the genre as firmly as her narrator locks herself into the hotel wardrobe from whose safe confines she hears the voice of danger, the writer hurries through the confessions and explanations of the dénouement with no sense of pride or satisfaction, to discard the whole business with a curt, '... and I never saw them again.' The borrowed narrative had served its purpose of allowing Jill to discover the limitations of the form, and to articulate an agenda for herself based on danger, safety and control.

Control is also a key theme of *The Children's Party*, written as a GCSE assignment five years later.

The children's party

It's eight o'clock and all the children have gone, trust me to be lumbered with the clearing away. First of all the living room. I think it wasn't a very good idea to let them use silly string; most of it has been trodden into the carpet with the crisps. I especially shouldn't have given a whole can of it to that boy who lives down the road; most of that ended up down the girls' backs and in the boys' eyes.

Well, now that's finished I'll tidy the dining room, this is the worst room of all. The table is like a wild jungle of food and drink. The once white table cloth has now been given a few splashes of colour to remind me how Bobby was squirting orange juice through his straw. Bobby has also kindly put orange spots over my once pure white dining-room wall. The atmosphere is so different in here now from just a couple of hours ago. It is so quiet, so heavenly quiet after the screams of six and seven year olds as they get orange juice squirted in their faces and egg rolls pushed down their backs.

It had all started quite reasonably really, not too noisy, but then Bobby started doing his straw and egg roll tricks and of course the other children started doing things back and I quickly removed all the cocktail sticks when they began to be used as weapons. As I was the only supervisor I was finding it more and more difficult to control twenty screaming orange and egg stained six year olds. My screaming at them to be quiet couldn't be heard, so I went into the kitchen, picked up the metal tea tray and banged it with a wooden spoon. The result was like magic: all twenty heads turned one way at once, their mouths wide open, staring at this adult who had apparently gone mad. After the food we played the usual party games. These went reasonably well apart from 'pass the parcel' where there were a few arguments over who was holding the parcel when the music stopped. So after the games I put some music on for the children to dance to; 'nothing can be wrong with a dance,' I thought. But how wrong can someone get! The girls were fairly well behaved, but the boys! Their idea of dancing was to see who could jump up and down and make the most noise with their feet on the floor. After a quarter of an hour of continuous thumping the parents started to arrive. 'Thank goodness,' I thought, 'Freedom at last.'

I was very surprised when I heard a conversation between one parent and son: 'Did you have a nice time, dear?' 'Yes, it was really good, the best party I've been to.'

I will never forget that boy's face, a picture of happiness, although I am sure his mother won't be tonight when she finds all that squashed egg stuck to his back!

All the children seem to have enjoyed it, I can not believe it. I'm sure when I was six years old my ideal party was not having egg put down my back, orange squirted in my face and pass fifteen minutes away stamping on crisps and silly string, and also go home with marks on my arms where the person next to me thought I needed an injection with a cocktail stick. Never mind, that is the next generation for you.

The central section of *The Children's Party* is structurally similar to that of *The Mystery of the Castle*: the narrator takes an initiative (pretending to be sick, banging the tray) to gain control of the situation, then relinquishes control to authority figures (the police, the children's parents). In both cases she describes her own assigned role ('she's only a kid, I was the only supervisor'), and describes herself as she is perceived by other people in the narrative ('the wretched child, this adult who had apparently gone mad').

In most other respects, *The Children's Party* displays measurable advances in linguistic complexity and sophistication. *The Mystery of the Castle* contains no premodified noun phrases of the descriptive density of 'my once pure white dining-room wall, his straw and egg roll tricks' or 'twenty screaming orange and egg stained six year olds.' The range and variety of combination of clauses is wider in *The Children's Party*: 'all twenty heads turned one way at once, their mouths wide open, staring at this adult who had apparently gone mad.' Jill chooses a challenging timeframe: the narrator is reflecting on the events of the party just past and on some of its present effects while clearing up. Most of the narrative moves easily between present ('It's eight o'clock'), perfect ('the children have gone'), past ('it wasn't a very good idea ...'), the immediate future from the point of view of the narrative present ('I'll tidy the dining room'), pluperfect ('It had all started ...'), progressive ('I was finding it more and more difficult ...'). Jill also refers to the more distant future from the point of view of the narrative present with 'I will never forget that boy's face ...' and to the more distant past of her own childhood with 'when I was six years old ...'. At these points her control of coherence across clauses dislocates:

> I will never forget that boy's face, a picture of happiness, although I am sure his mother won't be tonight ...

> I'm sure when I was six years old my ideal party was not having egg put down my back, orange squirted in my face and pass fifteen minutes away stamping on crisps and silly string, and also go home with marks on my arms ...

These minor discontinuities are themselves evidence of progress; Jill is willing to experiment with grammatical structures of increasing variety and complexity to express contrasts and to accumulate key clauses because she is able to work outwards from a comfortable stance. The account of the children's party itself, including the use of direct speech, is framed by the narrator's speaking voice. She notices details of the mess, recalls events, draws lessons from the experience, contrasts the chaotic event with the peaceful aftermath, reflects on her own role and responses, compares her charges' behaviour with that of her own at their age.

The tone of all but the central part of the narrative is characteristic of speech, with enclitic forms ('it's, wasn't, shouldn't, that's, I'll, I'm'), assumptions of shared reference ('that boy who lives down the road, Bobby'), minor sentences and clauses ('First of all the living room, but the boys!') and colloquial expressions ('trust me, lumbered, well, really, of course, never mind'). Whereas Jill's 'adventures' in *The Mystery of the Castle* took place in the context of the specious security of a half-assimilated written genre, the more dependable base of her own language experience in *The Children's Party* allows her to move freely and adventurously into the demanding syntax of the written mode safe in the knowledge that she can return to the familiar forms of spoken anecdote.

The implicit model of language which pupils and students bring to their own language use is clearly a vital component in their language development, and to diminish any part of it is to curtail potential for growth. Until recently, spoken language has been given limited attention by schools and colleges, reducing pupils' and students' scope for tentative, exploratory, interactional thinking. As a consequence, pupils and students have found themselves obliged to carry out these sensitive cognitive operations through the altogether less flexible medium of writing. Their task is even more burdensome if they have to work within the constraints of stereotyped versions of speaking ('casual', 'sloppy', 'unstructured') and writing ('formal', 'rigorous', 'structured'). As national and regional projects and the National Curriculum commitment to speaking and listening begin to exert their influence on departmental schemes of work, richer learning contexts will be created so that learners are enabled to draw openly on progressively wider and deeper aspects of their language experience. The shift in attitudes necessary to achieve this does not require us to demote literacy, or literature, but to enlarge our conception of the place of language in learning.

4 Developing schemes of work

National Curriculum requirements and examination syllabuses can lay heavy on attempts to develop schemes of work for language awareness. The English National Curriculum is issue-based, and may become assessment-led, deterring some departments from the more desirable open, exploratory, investigative approaches based on pupils' and students' language experience. English departments which stress response to literature and systematic, resource-based methods may find it difficult to integrate the so-called 'Knowledge About Language' strand into existing departmental schemes. There is a constant danger that texts become illustrations of language study concepts rather than points of departure for investigating language.

Serendipity can play a part in generating investigations, particularly for a teacher whose mind-set is prepared for opportunities as they arise. For example, in the course of reading aloud some stories written by Year 8 pupils, the phrase 'our Albert' was used. I took the opportunity to consider this dialect usage, and wrote this minimal sentence pair on the board and asked pupils for their responses:

> I'm going to see Albert.
> I'm going to see our Albert.

One pupil claimed that 'Saying *our Albert* is just being lazy.' Another developed the theme: 'People in the south speak properly and say *Albert*, but people in the north are lazy and say *our Albert*.' One pupil, uneasy perhaps with this general denigration of Northerners, expressed the tolerant liberal line that 'They are just different ways of speaking.' Another, listening in disbelief to this value-ridden nonsense, pointed out that '*Our Albert* tells you that Albert is a brother or something.'

Prompted by this discussion, a pupil new to the school and to the area mentioned her puzzlement at first hearing the term 'barmcake', a local word for a small bread roll. From their own experience the rest of the pupils in the class offered similar terms which they had encountered:

baps, batches, cobs, crusties, dunkies, lizzies, muffins, rolls, stovies

I asked the pupils to think about why there are so many words for small bread rolls used in different areas of the UK when there is only one common word – 'loaf' – for a large loaf of bread. Various reasons were suggested:

- Small rolls are made in lots of different ways, whereas a loaf is basically the same everywhere.
- Some of the different words for small rolls tell you something about them. For example, batches are so called because they are baked in sets of twelve or twenty-four all stuck together; 'crusties' have a crunchy crust.
- People used to make their own small rolls, so they thought it was alright to call them what they wanted. Larger loaves are usually made by bakers or large firms, so they all call them by the same word.

A pupil mentioned that young people have their own words for sweets in different parts of the country, such as 'grots' and 'totties', whereas adults just call them 'sweets.' Another fastened on different words for the narrow alleyway between two rows of terraced houses, for example 'ginnel', 'entry', 'gitty', 'sidepass'.

Literary texts can also provide opportunities for exploration of meanings and usage in controllable contexts. Many departmental schemes of work already use the rich resource of riddles as ways into poetry, and these can also encourage that lively openness to meaning which is essential for pupils' enjoyment of language. Three simple examples are as follows:

What runs but never walks? (A river)
What is put on a table and cut, but never eaten? (A pack of cards)
What has teeth but cannot bite? (A comb)

These riddles exploit interrelations between words and contexts which can easily be developed, for instance by discovering other contexts for the terms:

to run – a bath
        – an organization
        – a computer programme
run–down – applied to a building
            – applied to a person
to run someone down – in a car
                    – by criticizing them

The difference in meaning and sentence structure between:

She ran up a hill.
She ran up a bill.

Compounds such as

> a fun–run
> an also–ran
> a non–runner
> a run–in
> a runabout

Idioms such as

> to give someone the runaround
> to give someone the run of the place
> to tell someone to take a running jump

However, opportunism has its limits, and while nobody wants to enslave pupils to National Curriculum requirements, it would be reassuring to know that these could be met in the process of achieving wider aims. One possible approach is to base schemes of work loosely on texts, literary and non-literary, spoken and written, to create a framework for activitating issues and generating investigations, and to provide a link between the issue-based demands of syllabuses, schemes of work and assessment frameworks, such as the National Curriculum, and pupils' own experience of and ideas about language. For example, consider this extract from an early attempt, written by a journalist, to address issues about people's attitudes to language:

> 'I think her pad is the most, way out, absolutely fab,' the girl in the train said excitedly to her friend. 'It's yooky.'
> The man in the corner winced.
> 'Why can't they talk English?' he whispered angrily to me. I see him occasionally in the train, but I don't know his name. We nod and most times travel in silence, but every so often we talk about this and that during the journey.
> 'But that is English,' I said.
> 'Well, if that's English, I give up,' he replied fiercely. 'That rubbish?'
> 'It stands as good a chance of being in the English dictionary as any other of the words we are using to each other.'
> 'Talk sense,' he growled. 'Can you imagine "fab" being in the English dictionary?'
> 'With no trouble at all. If we had been in a stagecoach two hundred years ago you might have been saying to me now "Can you imagine 'mob' being in the English dictionary?" '
> 'But that's different. You've got to have some standards. You can't have any slang and teenage gimmick word being called English.'
> 'You are saying that slang is not English?'
> 'Well, not good English.'

This text raises issues such as the vocabulary associated with younger speakers and the status of dictionaries as a source of authority in language which might be used as a basis for discussion in fulfilling the National Curriculum requirement to:

> Reading Level 6: Show in discussion of their reading an awareness that words can change in use and meaning over time and demonstrate some of the reasons why.

But discussion might mean no more than an opportunity for pupils to air prejudices, so their understanding of these issues also requires the discipline of empirical investigation. At one level, this might mean pupils thinking of their own examples of words which they use but their parents don't. Or pupils might gather examples in notebooks over the course of a week, perhaps working with adults, including parents, to gain another perspective on their use. Making a systematic glossary of terms reveals in a practical way some of the problems faced by dictionary compilers, and gives pupils a critical standpoint for seeing a dictionary as a description of a lexicon rather than a seal of approval for accepted or standard usage.

Other issues go beyond empirical investigation, being drawn from the evaluative and explanatory frameworks which people in any language community need to make sense of their language experience. They involve issues which students must think through if they are to engage in language study in any meaningful sense, but cannot be addressed by simply collecting terms and devising glossaries. These include:

Liberal and conservative attitudes to language use
Pejorative and subjective judgements of language
Changes in attitudes to language use

Discussion could fulfil the following National Curriculum requirements:

> Speaking and Listening Level 10: Show ... an awareness of the factors that influence people's attitudes to the way other people speak.

> Reading Level 10: Demonstrate ... some understanding of attitudes in society towards language change ...

Text-centred approaches to the early stages of language awareness and language study can offer the possibility of constant feedback between theoretical frameworks and pupils' and students' own empirical investigations into how language is used. When this dialectic gets under way, students may select a *focus* on the text under discussion and use it as a source of *data* for developing *theories* about their selected aspect of language, derived either from their own ideas, or from language study and linguistics, perhaps mediated by the teacher. Data and theories together may then suggest further texts and lines of investigation, and so the process continues, continually widening and enriching learners' understanding of language. In diagrammatic form, the system may look something like this:

Underlying structure for a scheme of work in language awareness and language study

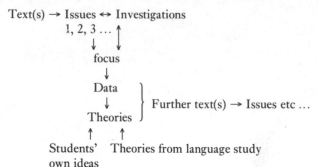

This process can be illustrated at any level, from a group of primary pupils talking about two or three different versions of a folk tale to a theoretical linguist investigating the finer points of verb phrase structure. For the purpose of this book, examples will be given from texts and responses at 11–16 and at 16+, the contexts being Key Stage 3 (the early secondary years) of the National Curriculum and Language Study for A Level English Language at 16+ respectively.

Example 1   KAL Key Stage 3

Catherine's Skiing Trip

Text(s)
The text for consideration is an extract from a long transcript recorded during a lesson in which Year 9 pupils talked to the class informally and with little preparation about recent events in their lives. Catherine's account of a school trip abroad followed a straight chronological line from the departure of the coach to its return.

Catherine's Skiing Trip

the first day skiing went OK but all the advanced skiers did fall over – and um – I expect all the beginners did as well – but the skiing was really good and the sun was out of the – and that first night we all had a disco and – right – the second day's skiing was really good – and I think everyone was a bit more able to ski and then that night I think we went swimming – and the next day it was skiing again – that was really good – and there was some men on who was skiing – a few people got hurt – Totie broke her arm – a couple of people got concussion – and – Elaine did her hip in – and – ur – Neil did his ear in – um – and quite a few other people got hurt – Helen did her knee in – otherwise it was really good – and then the last night we had the ski presentation – that was absolutely fantastic – I had too much to dr – I think about all of us had a bit too much to drink – that was really good – I had a row with Mr S. and told him where to go – it was brill

Issues

Language issues raised in the monologue *Catherine's Skiing Trip* include (i) *features of informal talk* and (ii) *grammar*

Data

Informal talk Focusing on the features of language we might expect in a stretch of informal talk may enable pupils to identify examples from *Catherine's Skiing Trip* of *informal words and phrases, repetitions, unfinished sentences and phrases, voiced and unvoiced pauses*, perhaps producing such data as the following:

Features of informal talk

Informal words and phrases	*Repetitions*	*Pauses*	
		Voiced	*Unvoiced*
... went OK	really good	and um (line $\frac{1}{2}$)	(lines 2, 3 etc.)
a bit more able to	did ... in	and ur (line 8)	
there was some men	too much to drink	um (line 9)	
on			
Totie [a nickname?]			
did ... in			
about all of us			
brill			

Grammar Pupils' focus on the grammatical structures in *Catherine's Skiing Trip* might include exploration of the range of *sentence-connectors* used, and of some of the most commonly *repeated syntactic patterns*.

It is tempting to suggest that an informal spoken text uses 'and' as the main sentence-connector, and therefore to imply that the narrative structure is somehow simpler than an equivalent written text. In fact 'and' is used liberally in *Catherine's Skiing Trip*, but there is a wider range of connectors than this. For example, lexical connectors like 'and', 'but', 'then' are often associated with an unvoiced pause, and many sentences are connected with an unvoiced pause only, or are not connected by a pause or a lexical item at all, but by factors which do not emerge in a broad transcript, such as changes in intonation indicating a new tone group – perhaps the nearest spoken equivalent to a full stop. The variety of connectors, including combinations of lexical connectors, pauses and intonation (symbolized as INT), become clearer if the sentences and their connectors are separated out:

Catherine's Skiing Trip: sentence-connectors

Sentence	Sentence-connector(s)
the first day skiing went OK	but
all the advanced skiers did fall over	– and um –
I expect all the beginners did as well	– but
the skiing was really good	and
the sun was out of the	– and
that first night we all had a disco	and –
right – the second day's skiing was really good	– and
I think everyone was a bit more able to ski	and then
that night I think we went swimming	– and
the next day it was skiing again	– INT
that was really good	– and
there was some men on who was skiing	– INT
a few people got hurt	– INT
Totie broke her arm	– INT
a couple of people got concussion	– and –
Elaine did her hip in	– and –
ur – Neil did his ear in	– um – and
quite a few other people got hurt	– INT
Helen did her knee in	– otherwise
it was really good	– and then
the last night we had the ski presentation	– INT
that was absolutely fantastic	– INT
I had too much to dr –	INT
I think about all of us had a bit too much to drink	– INT
that was really good	– INT
I had a row with Mr S.	and
told him where to go	– INT
it was brill	

A count of the type of sentence-connectors shows nearly as many uses of intonation, some supported by an unvoiced pause and some not, as of 'and'.

Investigations

Informal talk On the basis of the data *Features of Informal Talk*, pupils might consider further transcripts of informal speech, perhaps from other pupils, or from older speakers. A class might record and transcribe its own collection of informal spoken accounts, exploring how typical these features are of spoken discourse. They might compare the spoken versions to accounts written for a variety of purposes.

Grammar Further analysis of the data on sentence-connectors in *Catherine's Skiing Trip* at Key Stage 3 would probably be inappropriate, though there is plenty of scope for it. For example, one connector, 'otherwise', connects a sequence of sentences to a final evaluation. Most of the uses of 'and' occur either before a time-indicator, such as 'that first night', 'the next day' and so on, or within the tightly cohesive list of injuries which Catherine conveys with such relish. If we consider the account as falling into natural divisions or episodes, each rounded off with an evaluation such as 'that was really good', we can see that these sections tend to begin with a pause and a change of intonation rather than an explicit lexical marker such as 'and'.

Pupils' own investigations would be more likely to focus on recordings of anecdotes from their own language experience, in which the apparently simple process of transcription raises these, and other, issues.

Theories

Informal talk   Pupils' own explanations of the data in *Features of Informal Talk* might include such factors as:

The personality of the speaker
The fact that the speaker knows, and shares terms of reference with, her audience
The purposes of this talk: to convey a sense of enjoyment and to communicate information

Relevant theoretical frameworks from language study might include the idea of levels of formality and the idea of language use as an index of peer group identity.

Grammar   Approaching grammatical theory with Key Stage 3 pupils can be daunting, but there is no reason why previous generations' errors, including over-analysis, should be repeated. In the case of *Catherine's Skiing Trip*, one concept and two grammatical operations can tell us much about how the text works. Pupils at this stage can recognize *similar syntactic patterns*, example sentences in which one word or phrase is *expanded*, or in which a word or phrase is *substituted*. For example:

Similar syntactic patterns

1	Elaine	did her hip in	
	Neil	did his ear in	
	Helen	did her knee in	
2	the skiing		was really good
	the second day's skiing		was really good
3		I	had	too much to dr –
	I think	all of us	had a bit	too much to drink

(1) represents an obvious syntactic similarity, with substitutions of noun phrases in the subject and object position. In (2), the speaker repeats a

syntactic frame to move her narrative forward by expanding the noun phrase in the subject position. In (3) the speaker expands both the subject and object noun phrases to spread responsibility and ameliorate the effect of her admission. She also embeds the expanded sentence in a higher order clause, 'I think ...', perhaps to stress the subjectivity of her judgement, and to enhance the conspiratorial sense.

Further text(s) → issues etc. ...
Both in terms of informal talk and grammar, other texts for pupils to consider in the light of their explorations of *Features of Informal Talk* and of the relations between overall structure and purposes and grammar might include recordings of anecdotes and exchanges, transcripts, written representations of dialogue, for example in prose and drama.

Example 2   16+ A Level English Language

Isle of Man seafarers

The text is an extract from a conversation between a retired inshore fisherman (R. S.) and a retired ferry skipper (W. W.), both from the Isle of Man. The focus of the book from which this extract was taken is the language of work, and the intended readership is non-specialist, so the author has employed a slightly adapted form of the orthodox English writing system.

Text(s)

Isle of Man seafarers

R. S.:   Light-moon flood, and the mate took the dark-moon ebb. I'd – I'd a good experience o' that.
W. W.: Oh, it were ...
R. S.:   Blackest watch o' the lot.
W. W.: There's none of 'em cared about the dark-moon ebb, but they all liked the light-moon.
R. S.:   Oh, aye. Oh, I know we – we had a do once in the – er – in the *Desdemonia*. Old John Nutall was – you knowed Old John?
W. W.: Oh, yes, I noo him.
R. S.:   Well, we were running down from – we were running along Laxey – er – past Laxey, making fer Ramsey Bay, an' it were blowing hard an' we'd two reeves [horizontal portions of a sail which may be folded to make it smaller in rough weather] in, and Old John happened to put his tiller a little bit o' one side an' over the mainsail came, broke all the reef-ear-rings [rings in a sail, used for attaching a rope to fold the sail. A term unrecorded in the *Oxford English Dictionary*], an' then we'd full sail on. Then we had to down with all the lot of

it on deck until we got our reef-ear-rings made all right. We once –
once in – er – in Laxey Bay there, we once picked a little lad up
i't'net.

W. W.: Aye?

R. S.: Aye! An', we had a do at Peel one time in these nick – er – they call
'em nickies [two-masted Manx herring-drifters], don't they?

W. W.: Yis.

R. S.: Two masts, going a-herring fishing: One of 'em, he couldn't get in, he
didn't know where he was, an' we went to his rescue an' fetched him
in ... . On a Saturday night, when we come in from sea, Church
Street used to be our place, silk velvet wesket on, blue Devon jackets
an' weskets, an' a velvet collar on your jacket, and there we used to
stand, discussin' where the best place was for fishin'. Women used to
ask their husbands, 'Where have you been?' 'Oh, I've been i'th'Ole'
or 'I've been on t'Showd' or 'I've been on t'Slaughter [names of
fishing grounds in the Irish Sea]'. On t'Slaughter we – er – used to go
for – er – ray, plenty of good ray, an' in the 'Ole we used to get cod,
an' on t'Showd we used to get plaice-flukes an' gurnets [gurnards, a
kind of fish] and that. But we used to have to sort it out. Yellow
gurnets an' plaice went as prime, grey gurnets went as offals, they
didn't – only – er – so many a basket. Yellow gurnets an' plaice were
sold so much a score, in weight, but ray an' that were sold by so much
a basket, so was grey gurnets, so was dogfish.

W. W.: Aye.

R. S.: Oysters were sold at ...

W. W.: They counted 'em.

R. S.: ... at – er – seven an' six a hundred. Seven an' six a hundred fer –
fer – er – oysters, but you used to have to give good count, one to
every quarter. There were four oysters over the hundred every time,
an' little oysters, well, they were kept in a bag separate. Them was –
er – always divided between the crew, er – that would be stocker [fish
of other kinds taken when fishing for herring or pilchards. A sum of
money accruing to a member of the crew as his share in this].

Issues

Some of the issues raised by this passage include: (i) *language interaction*, (ii)
sharing experiences, (iii) *features of spoken English*, (iv) *representation of speech
in writing*, (v) *occupational lexis* and (vi) *regional dialect*.

Data

Language interaction   Focusing first on the language interactions represented goes some way to taking the conversation on its own terms, since part
of the point of the exchange from the speakers' point of view is the relationship between their contributions. In extracting data on this issue, students
might observe:

- R. S. finishes W. W.'s sentence for him

  W. W.: Oh, it were ...
  R. S.: Blackest watch o' the lot.

- R. S. and W. W. agree with each other; for example:

  R. S.: Oh, aye
  W. W.: Oh, yes
  W. W.: Aye

- R. S. and W. W. pick up phrases from each other; for example:

  R. S.: Light-moon flood ... dark-moon ebb ...
  W. W.: ... the dark-moon ebb ... the light-moon
  W. W.: They counted 'em.
  R. S.: ... a good count ...

- R. S. and W. W. ask and answer questions; for example:

  R. S.: ... they call 'em nickies, don't they?
  W. W.: Yis.

Students' own investigations might include their own recording and transcribing, together with attempts to produce a written script of an exchange
which sounds like natural speech when read aloud. Relevant theories from
Linguistics might include *discourse analysis, conversational analysis* and
ethnomethodological approaches. Students' own concerns might include the
relationship between R. S. and W. W.

Sharing experiences   For the purpose of focusing on this issue, students
might divide the exchange into sections, correlating each anecdote or experience with some of the names, technical terms and local or dialectal terms
which provide the speakers with shared terms of reference. For example:

Description of section	Names	Technical terms	Local or dialectal terms
1 Losing the mainsail	the *Desdemonia* John Nutall Laxey Ramsey Bay	reeves reef-ear-rings	to down with ... it
2 Rescuing the nickie	Peel	nickies	nickies
3 Saturday night out	Church Street		
4 Reports of fishing trips	th'Ole t'Showd t'Slaughter		
5 Accounts of fish caught + weighing, measuring, pricing	t'Slaughter th'Ole t'Showd		stocker

Students might develop this issue by investigating differences between the ways in which 'experts' discuss a topic among themselves and how they might explain it to an outsider. Theories from Linguistics might include discussion of so-called *antilanguages*, such as *underworld argot*, and the language of students' own peer groups.

Features of spoken English Students who have already investigated spoken English through recording and transcribing may recognize several characteristic features of speech in this passage, including the following:

- Repetitions

  R. S.: ... I'd – I'd ...

- Self-corrections

  R. S.: Well, we were running down from – we were running along Laxey – er – past Laxey ...

- Self-interruptions

  R. S.: ... Old John Nutall was – you knowed Old John?

- Pauses and hesitations

  R. S.: Them was – er – always divided between the crew, er – that would be stocker.

- Unfinished sentences

  R. S.: ... they didn't – only – er – so many a basket

For their own investigations, students might examine which 'features of speech' characterize a range of types of unscripted English, including casual conversation, monologue, narrative and explanation. Useful theoretical ideas include the distinction between *context-dependence* and *autonomy* in language use. Students' own ideas might emerge from their speculations on the reasons for some of the features mentioned above; for example, trying to differentiate between different reasons for pauses and hesitations in speech.

Representation of speech in writing Focus on some of the means used to represent speech with the limited resources of the orthodox writing system might allow students to identify the following data:

Dashes (–) and 'er's to represent unvoiced and voiced pauses

Commas, full stops, exclamation marks and question marks to indicate likely patterns of intonation

Apostrophes to give some indication of likely pronunciations of words and phrases

Discussion of the limitations of this representation of speech shows how stylized it is. A few selected features are used to give an impression of pronunciation. For example, apostrophes are used to mark 'o', an', i't'' and ''Ole', but the following words and phrases are spelled quite conventionally:

Orthodox spelling	Likely pronunciation	Possible spelling
blowing hard	/blƏυωιn αd/	blowin' 'ard
mainsail	/meιnsƏl/	mainsel
they didn't	/δι dιnt/	thi' di'nt

Students can discover for themselves the artificiality of writing systems which attempt to convey the subtleties of pronunciations by devising their own ways of representing speech as accurately as possible. The relevant area of Linguistics is *phonetics and phonology*, and students might be introduced to the idea of using a single written symbol to represent each separate phoneme or speech sound in English.

Occupational lexis   Focus on this issue might produce data in the form of terms from the passage related to four or five categories. For example:

Seafaring generally	Terms relating to boats	Types of fish	Measurements	Others
light-moon flood	reeves	ray	a basket	stocker
mate	tiller	cod	a score	
dark-moon ebb	mainsail	plaice-flukes		
watch	reef-ear-rings	gurnets		
running down	deck	yellow gurnets		
running along	nickies	grey gurnets		
full sail	masts	dogfish		
net		oysters		

Discussion of these data might lead students to investigate terms and categories from an occupational variety with which they are familiar, perhaps in consultation with a family member or acquaintance. The relevant theoretical framework from Linguistics is the idea of register, but students may have their own ideas about the origins and uses of technical and other occupational terms.

Regional dialect   Regional dialect, defined in terms of geographical variation in lexis and grammar, can be a central focus in the early stages of language study because it raises so many important issues about attitudes to language, and offers an accessible introduction to some of the more technical aspects of language study, including grammar. In this passage, the number of distinctly regional words is limited to 'aye', 'lad' and 'stocker', but the range of grammatical variation is wide, as these data suggest:

Characteristic grammatical structure	Grammatical focus
it were	subject–verb relationship
There's none of 'em cared	tense
knowed/noo	verb morphology
running down from along past	prepositions
it were blowing hard	subject–verb relationship
a little bit o' one side	prepositional usage
we had to down with … it	verb usage
going a-herring fishing	'a-' marking the whole phrase 'herring fishing' as a single lexical item
when we come in	verb tense
i' th'Ole on t'Showd on t'Slaughter	prepositions
Them was	subject–verb relationship

In the early stages pupils and students might profitably investigate people's attitudes to these and other grammatical structures.

Extending a scheme of work

It would clearly be impossible to outline a full scheme of work for language awareness, but it may be useful to suggest how a department might develop and organize resources for one relevant part of the English National Curriculum. I will focus on the KAL strand of the *Speaking and Listening* component, and I will assume a mixed ability Year 9 class, able to work successfully in groups, as a whole class and individually, accustomed to oral work, including discussion and roleplay, and with a strong creative and investigative spirit.

In the course of their English work for Years 7 and 8, this class will have taken part in discussions on a range of topics, shared experiences through anecdotes, interviewed each other for mock chat shows, perhaps interviewed teachers and other adults, administered questionnaires, persuaded, instructed and informed each other in roleplays, improvised peer group and family conflicts, and given both planned and spontaneous formal presentations to the whole class. Some of this oral work will have been recorded and played back, some of it perhaps transcribed.

Among the recordings was *Catherine's Skiing Trip*, and the class has discussed the issues of 'informal talk' and 'grammar', derived data about 'informal words', 'repetitions' and 'pauses' and related these to their own theories about levels of formality and peer-group language, and identified the sentence-connectors, working in groups to solve problems of syntactic patterning. As part of their own investigations they have recorded and transcribed other anecdotes, among them one also related to the topic of skiing holidays:

> um – my mum's friend – she went skiing – with a load of other friends – and um – she was – she – she needed the loo desperately she was – there was no toilets around – she had one of these all in one – suits – and um – so – they – she found a log – and she went behind this log – and she couldn't see so she was holding on to urm – the wire where – the learner skis are – and this man went past – and he pulled her out – and she came flying out [laughter] and she had nothing on [laughter] she had nothing on and this ski suit it's flapping behind her and – so – she said right – I can't stay in that hotel now everyone's seen me – so she went to this other hotel – and urm she was waiting for some of her friends and urm – she met this man and he had a broken arm – and they got talking and she asked him how did you break his arm and he says – he says you won't believe me she goes – try me – and ur – he goes well I was on one of those – ski lifts – and I saw this woman skiing with nothing on [laughter] so I turned round to have a better look and I fell off and broke my arm [laughter]

The framework used to discuss *Catherine's Skiing Trip* is also applicable to this anecdote. The informal words, repetitions and pauses all have a part to play in conveying the story effectively. Use of the narrative present – 'he says', 'she goes', 'he goes' – and of 'this' for indefinite reference in 'this log', 'this man', 'this other hotel', are conventional features of informal jocular narrative. But a significant difference is that whereas Catherine's account was first-hand, this anecdote has been processed through other speakers – the mum's friend, then perhaps the mum, then the pupil. It belongs, in fact, to that fund of stories which help to define and enrich the experience of belonging to a family. So pupils' own investigations emerging from this text might involve tactful research with parents or caregivers and other relatives and acquaintances to explore some of the ways in which family groups are held together by the experiences and values which such accounts contain.

A further contribution, in the form of a spoken narrative text, comes from a long interview with a lady from the Manchester area, Miss Cooper, undertaken as part of an Oral History project. Miss Cooper's mother was an active member of the suffragette movement, and often spoke to large crowds on the issue of women's franchise. This particular story from Manchester Polytechnic Oral History Unit concerns a visit by Mrs Cooper to speak in Hull:

Mrs Cooper's speech

Miss Cooper: well this is – she went to Hull to speak to the fishermen you see – at the docks you see – and everyone made fun of suffragettes – it didn't matter whether they were – ur – old or young you see

Interviewer: it's still the same now

Miss Cooper: yes of course it is – and they skit about it don't they – and I think – you know – it's best to take the dignified way – anyway she went to Hull and she had to get up very early in the morning – once I was staying at Cleethorpes with her and she took me there – to show me – show me where she went you see – and she – and all these men – there was this auction of fish on you see – and they met her – to her alarm – well she usually got antagonism – well they met her – and – escorted her – to this dock – and she thought there was something fishy about this – fishy yes well – well they kept live fish in tanks with lids on – for the hotels you know – anyhow they took my mother and they said *We've got a platform ready for you Mrs Cooper* – they knew her name because it was all on the – my mother was a strong woman you know – she was taller than me – she'd be five foot seven – and broad built – and they took her on – onto it – and she thought *There's something fishy about this* and she started speaking – and – and – it started – the lid started to coming up

Interviewer: that she was standing on?

Miss Cooper: yes and she she stood on it to sort of hold it and – ur – there were bass in it – live bass

Interviewer: jumping?

Miss Cooper: ready to take to hotels – and anyhow she stood it – they clapped her like mad when she'd finished because she'd stuck to it

This text raises new issues and new directions for research and investigation. Miss Cooper uses this account to express important values; 'the dignified way' and the importance of sticking to the task even when you are being made fun of, and her admiration for her mother. The story itself begs to be acted out, with the fish sellers planning their attempt to demean Mrs Cooper, and her speech from the top of the tank full of live fish the central language event. The department may have access to other texts relevant to language study: copies of posters, speeches, tracts, biographies.

In the course of discussing and investigating these three texts, pupils would have touched on many of the National Curriculum requirements, including *non-standard English*, the significance of *purpose* (sharing experiences) and *audience* (peers for the pupils' accounts, an interviewer for Miss Cooper), *tone of voice* (what tone of voice might be appropriate for 'she had nothing on and this ski suit it's flapping behind her'?), *types of spoken communication* (anecdotes, conversations, political speeches), *attitudes* to the way other people speak (how might the fish sellers' responses to Mrs Cooper change as her speech progressed?).

The direction for the scheme of work after this point would depend on the needs of pupils and on the department's organization and traditions. Some departments might prefer to pick up the themes through literature, using texts based on family experiences. Others might prefer to develop the possibilities for writing. Whatever line is taken, pupils can bring with them the security and esteem of knowing that their own language experience and expertise has been valued as the basis for their activities and studies.

5 English language study at 16+

The first realistic suggestions for syllabuses in English Language at Advanced level were made in the late 1970s more or less simultaneously by a group of teachers represented by George Keith of North Cheshire College in Warrington and from another group whose spokesperson was Dennis Freeborn from the College of Ripon and York St John in York. Dennis Freeborn's group worked with the London Board to develop its distinctive syllabus, while George Keith's approached The Joint Matriculation Board, who agreed to set up a working party to design a syllabus and establish administrative structures. This chapter will be concerned exclusively with the JMB A Level English Language syllabus because that is the one with which I am most familiar. The first JMB A Level English Language courses started in 1983, with 209 students from a small group of schools and colleges in the Northwest and Derbyshire.

From the point of view of many of the teachers on the JMB Working Party, the syllabus was a response to a growing awareness that schools offered limited opportunities to students for their own writing after the age of 16, other than critical essays on the writings of others. Some A Level English Literature syllabuses offered an optional test in creative writing, but this was taken up by a small minority of students, and performance on this aspect of the syllabus did not affect the vital A Level grade. Also, the kind of writing expected was limited to the broadly 'creative' category, which in practice excluded much writing of the more practical and socially useful kind. The importance of a variety of writing opportunities for pupils' language development from the early days of schooling up to GCSE is generally acknowledged, so it seemed sensible to continue, develop and extend it after 16.

The other main strand in syllabus development derived from the increasing interest in language as a discipline of study which emerged first from Higher Education in the explosive growth of work in Linguistics, and the increasing use of its techniques and theoretical frameworks in a range of other disciplines. Pioneering work by M. A. K. Halliday in the early 1970s with the Schools Council Linguistics Project had shown that many aspects of language study were accessible to school pupils, and that a genuinely investigative approach to language by teachers and learners could help to widen and enrich language experience.

From the point of view of learning and assessment, these strands of the A Level English Language syllabus are expressed as the ability to use language effectively and the ability to understand what language is and how it works. Effective use of English is assessed by means of the Original Writing component, and a Case Study paper, where students are given source material 48 hours before the exam in which the questions are given. Understanding of language is assessed by means of a Project – an investigation of an aspect of language use chosen by the student – and a formal examination, Paper 1. Briefly, the structure is this:

Paper 1   A 3-hour formal exam paper covering aspects of knowledge about language.

Paper 2   A Case Study paper with source material given 48 hours before the exam, and questions given on the day of the exam.

Original Writing   A folio of writing appropriate to a variety of purposes and audiences representing work done during the course.

Project   An investigation into a language-based topic of the student's own choice.

The JMB's A Level English Language syllabus is consortium-based, and has a 50 per cent coursework component. Coursework is assessed initially by teachers and is moderated by a process of agreement trials and external moderation. For the purpose of agreement trials, schools and colleges are grouped into consortia, each of which meets at least twice each academic year.

For Paper 1 students answer one question from each of three sections.

Section A contains a choice of essay questions on theoretical issues about language.

Section B requires critical response to examples of literary passages.

Section C requires critical response to examples of non-literary material.

An example of a Section A question about Language and Society from the 1988 Paper 1, which, if taken together with the discussion about slang in Chapter 1, illustrates the potential for continuity between 11–16 and 16+ in terms of language awareness and language study, is as follows:

Language and society

Discuss what difficulties there might be in formulating an accurate definition of 'slang', and explain some of the attitudes held in society towards its use.

You may if you wish refer to the following data which consists of ten state-ments made by a group of 13-year-olds, and a selection of terms considered by the same group to be 'slang'.

(a) *Statements about slang*
 1 Slang is a lazy way of speaking.
 2 Slang is mainly used by young people.
 3 Slang is like an alternative language.
 4 Slang is used because people have different meanings.
 5 Slang is a new or up-to-date way of speaking.
 6 Slang is used when you do not want to be posh.
 7 Some people use slang in their jobs.
 8 Slang is used by some people to make them seem tough.
 9 Slang comes from people missing parts of words out.
10 Slang comes from people who don't know how to speak properly.

(b) *Terms considered to be slang*

kids = children
dunno = I don't know
yeah = yes
mam = mother
copper = policeman
butty = sandwich
grub = food
apples and pears = stairs
dog and bone = telephone
pop = soft fizzy drinks
skint = penniless
specs = spectacles
brill = expression of approval

hiya = hello
quid = pound
nick = steal or police station
oh aye = yes
flippin' 'eck = an exclamation
chuddy = chewing gum
grots = sweets
what? = pardon?
a grand = £1,000
Yank = American
goggle box = television
snazzy = smart in appearance

Paper 2 is a case study paper. The questions are given to students at the time of the examination itself, but source material, which the questions are based on, is given out 48 hours before the examination. Students read three sets of source material and answer one question on one set of material in the examination. Questions are in the form of tasks inviting candidates to inter-pret, adapt and re-present source material for specified purposes and audiences other than those originally intended. Material from the following sources is given to students two days before the examination. An outline example of a Paper 2 Case Study question is as follows:

Source material
A report from the Chief Executive of Greater Manchester Council Recreation
    and Arts committee
Excerpts from *Tourism in Greater Manchester*
Extracts from *Lancashire* in *The King's England* series, by Arthur Mee
An article about Worsley Old Hall in Salford, from a colour supplement
Extracts from *Industrial Archaeology of Lancashire* by Owen Ashmore
Extracts from *Portrait of Manchester* by Michael Kennedy

An article about Wigan Pier from a journal
A Greater Manchester Council booklet, *Museums and Art Galleries*
A map of the area

On the day of the examination the following task was offered for students to complete as part of a choice of three questions:

You have been employed by the North West Tourist Board to help promote tourism in the Greater Manchester area.

Your task is to produce a booklet for the guidance of motor tourists who have three days to spare and who are particularly interested in industrial archaeology e.g. buildings, machinery and sites which have survived from an earlier industrial age.

You need not concern yourself about hotel accommodation, which will be taken care of by another agency, nor include such details as entrance fees which will be provided on a separate leaflet.

You should draw up an itinerary of selected places of interest which a tourist could follow without difficulty and which would offer an interesting variety of sites and museums to visit.

Concentrate on giving clear instructions about your chosen locations and make your selection and use of background information lively and relevant.

You should assume that the users of your guide will want more than a route map. They will find it helpful to have their tour put in a context of interesting information.

Please remember that the material written by individual authors is copyright. You are free to draw on the material but if it is quoted too extensively it may make the cost of producing the guide prohibitive.

For the Original Writing part of the coursework component, students produce three pieces of writing, clearly differentiated in terms of audience and purpose. Most students submit one piece of fictional narrative to fulfil the requirements of writing to entertain, often using prose but sometimes adopting drama or radio/TV script format, taking advantage of the provision of a taped presentation as an acceptable alternative to one written piece. The category of writing to persuade produces a very wide range of texts, including letters to newspapers and journals, articles, pamphlets, debate speeches on such topics as the environment, smoking, education, animal rights, the Third World. Writing whose primary function is to inform has included journal articles, biography, radio scripts for educational programmes, often, but not always, aimed at readers younger than the students themselves. Writing for instructional purposes is chosen by a comparatively small number of students, partly because of the difficulties of maintaining an expert authorial stance, and partly because writing precise instructions for other than very simple activities proves to be very difficult. The key to the

Original Writing component of the syllabus is summed up in the *Moderator's Report* (1989):

> The more candidates are encouraged to treat the writing process as one whose finished product might genuinely appear in print or performance, the more likely it is that they will engage with their material and move away from the attitude that they are writing merely to fulfil the minimum requirements of this examination. Thoroughness, attention to detail, technical accuracy, meticulous presentation, painstaking redrafting and testing on the intended readership all characterize the best submissions in this component.

Students are also expected to write a commentary on how at least some of their pieces of writing were produced, including details of intended audience, purposes, drafting processes and responses from readers. Considerable weight is given to this. George Keith, Chair of the Board of Examiners for the syllabus, discussing the *first five years* of A Level English Language in the *Examiner's Report* (1989), writes:

> ... commentaries are activities in which students may learn about the nature and functions of language in very profound and experimental ways. Reflection on genre, sentence structure, rhetorical effects, textual coherence, or the use of metaphor are now quite common and constitute that kind of discovered knowledge that can inform more abstract learning and give analytic discussion in Paper 1 more conviction and energy.

The principle of empirical investigation is central to students' work in the Project (Investigation into Language Use) component of the coursework. In her review of the JMB A Level English Language syllabus for NATE's Post 14 Committee, Margaret Whiteley observes that

> The syllabus is, I think, a radical and welcome departure from what has been previously offered at this level. It follows consistently from the investigative and participatory courses now being encouraged by GCSE. And that is exactly what this syllabus is: an investigation by the student into how language works.

Empirical investigation is the explicitly stated point of the Project, which requires students to collect and comment on language data. But it is also the unstated underpinning of language theory undertaken for Paper 1 topics. At one level, the Project offers students an opportunity to apply some of the theoretical ideas they have learnt in their work for Paper 1 topics to such areas of language study as language acquisition and development, the language of newspapers, magazines, comics and advertisements, spoken discourse, attitudes to language, the way language is used by occupational groups. At another, it provides for considerable learning interaction between language theory and practice.

The standards required are set out by the *Moderator's Report* (1986):

> While each kind of topic has its own possible strengths and potential pitfalls, good projects in all categories were characterised by those features which

remain the crucial ingredients of an excellent piece of work: a definite purpose and direction, good data, an awareness of possible weaknesses in methods of data collection, manageable scope, an analysis which addresses itself squarely to the data, a sensitive appraisal of what has been found, a concise and clear writing style, and sensible and honest use of secondary sources, where appropriate.

There are strong links between this component of the syllabus and Paper 1. Students need to undertake practical investigations of language in order to appreciate theoretical ideas fully, but they also need sound and positive ideas about language to get real value from their investigations.

An example of the interrelationship between students' investigations and their understanding of relevant theoretical frameworks can be seen in students' responses to the topic of Language Acquisition. This is one of the areas specified for study for Paper 1, and also happens to be one of the more popular subjects for Project investigation. In many ways it is ideal: students can gather a body of data fairly easily; there is a wide range of publications on the topic, from the popular and accessible to the technical and esoteric; the topic demands some knowledge of most major areas of language study, including phonology, grammar and semantics. Students' analyses of language acquisition data are often markedly different before and after they have participated in practical observations of young children speaking. For example, the following is from *A Child's Learning of English*:

A selection of utterances by Sophie (2 years 4 months)

me want that	me want drink
me want your tea	want put milk in there
me want read that	me want house for Kate
her want a blankie [blanket]	you play snakes and ladders me
Mary come me	I got some those
baby in big bed	her can't see
what that?	why Jack come?
why those two nother things broke?	me took one box
our play that on floor	

At the beginning of an Advanced level course of language study, students tend to notice ways in which children's language differs from that of adults, so that comments such as the following are very much the norm:

Sophie can't tell the difference between 'me' and 'I'.
Sophie can't use prepositions consistently.
Sophie can't use modals, except for 'can't'.
Sophie can't form questions correctly.

In making these judgements, students match Sophie's utterances against adult usage, perhaps intuitively adopting the point of view of a caregiver whose main concern is to encourage Sophie to approximate more closely to a target form. As a result, the students find themselves adopting a deficiency model of Sophie's language forms which stresses what she cannot do. However, by the end of the course, students are more inclined to make observations such as the following:

- Sophie can use words in Subject–Verb–Object–Adverbial order, e.g.:

Subject	Verb	Object	Adverbial
me	want	drink	
our	play	that	on floor

- Sophie can substitute in sentence frames, e.g.:

me want $\begin{cases} \text{that} \\ \text{drink} \\ \text{read that} \end{cases}$

- Sophie can form a variety of complex noun phrases, e.g.:

Determiner + noun:	your tea ... a blankie ... some those
Adjective + noun:	big bed
noun *and* noun:	snakes and ladders
Determiner phrase + noun:	those two nother things

- Sophie can catenate verbs, e.g.:

want put milk in there
me want read that

The latter is clearly more fruitful as an investigation of language acquisition. By treating Sophie's utterances as evidence of competence, students are able to place the data in a wider scheme of development, with some clear avenues for further exploration. For example:

What different forms do Sophie's adverbials take?
What sentence frames besides 'me want –' does Sophie use?
How might adult caregivers encourage her to develop them?
Can Sophie be encouraged to develop her noun phrases, for instance by recombining elements such as determiner–adjective–noun, to form 'your big bed'?

The difference between these two approaches is crucial. It is not simply that the second uses more technical terminology than the first, but rather that the descriptive approach takes a language system on its own terms and uses a theoretical framework, which naturally includes technical references in the form of terminology, to establish the norms which help to define and distinguish that system, then uses those norms as a starting point for more detailed investigation. What has happened to the students between the beginning and the end of their course is not merely that they have acquired some technical terms, but that they have had opportunities to work and play with two- and three-year-old speakers, to converse with and record them, to listen to the recordings and discuss what is being said in its social and physical context, and therefore to have a reason to try to find a vocabulary which does justice to the complexity of developing language.

A phenomenon similar to the above can be observed in students' responses to regional dialect forms over the period of their studies. One of the most difficult problems of language study at this level is how to deploy students' existing understanding of language without at the same time activating the prejudices and folk linguistics which form such a large part of what passes for common sense about language. To some extent it is possible to counter negative attitudes with positive ones – to insist from the high ground of pedagogical authority that all dialects are equal linguistically, that grammar is a descriptive and not a prescriptive activity, that aesthetic judgements about regional accents are just so much linguistic superstition. But high ground is not necessarily the most secure. Liberal and tolerant attitudes about language which are not based firmly on empirical investigations of language use will be unlikely to withstand linguistic bigotry which has equipped itself with accurate references to language history and detailed factual information about phonological structures and patterns of grammatical usage.

Most A Level English Language students can accept early in their course that the grammatical patterns used by regional dialect speakers are as consistent as those used by Standard English speakers. But without a descriptive framework, they find themselves falling back on the use of the standard form as a norm or paradigm. For example, these utterances are from the interview with Miss Cooper referred to in Chapter 4.

she got across with Mrs Pankhurst did my mother
he was dizzy was Macdonald
she was speaking with Mrs Fawcett – she was the head of her suffrage
    society Mrs Fawcett
it was very true was that film that came

Students' immediate response to these data, if asked to comment on the grammatical structures represented, is to 'translate' them into formal Standard English:

my mother did not get on well with Mrs Pankhurst
Macdonald was dizzy
she was speaking with Mrs Fawcett – Mrs Fawcett was the head of her
    suffrage society
that film that came was very true

Assimilating the dialect structure to the standard form masks rather than exposes the similarity of structure between the four individual utterances, and reveals little about the syntax of the original utterances. The source of this reflex may lie in repeated exposure to exercises from English Language textbooks in which perfectly consistent and rule-governed patterns related to such issues as number concord in everyday spoken language use are realized as sentences unconnected by register or reference to any plausible textual coherence, and stigmatized on no other evident authority than the textbook writer's subjective preference.

The similarities of patterning which help to justify the assertion that grammatical structures used in Miss Cooper's regional form are consistent and rule-governed can be brought out more sharply by being expressed as a series of paradigms:

she	got across with	Mrs Pankhurst	did	my mother
he	was	dizzy	was	Macdonald
she	was	the head of her suffrage society		Mrs Fawcett
it	was	very true	was	that film that came

Some knowledge of classes of words would allow students to describe the structures explicitly, for example:

Pronoun	Verb	Adjective/noun phrase	(Verb)	Noun phrase
she	got across with	Mrs Pankhurst	did	my mother
he	was	dizzy	was	Macdonald
she	was	the head of her suffrage society		Mrs Fawcett
it	was	very true	was	that film that came

This kind of structural description is a step forward from an unthinking reduction to standard forms, but it is still of limited value if applied to processed data out of the context of discourse. For example, it would be easy to get the impression from looking at the isolated utterances from Miss Cooper's interview that the main feature of her speech is her employment of regional dialect structures. In fact, a consideration of a longer extract from her interview shows that what few 'dialect forms' she does use are very thinly spread throughout the discourse, and are hardly noticeable in the narrative flow. It requires a conscious decision on the part of the investigator to focus on this particular aspect, particularly when there are other interesting issues relating to language and memory, the way speakers order events and background explanations in their anecdotes, the significance of such features of spoken language as pauses, fillers, self-corrections, differences between speaking and writing. Here is Miss Cooper's account (from Manchester Polytechnic Oral History Unit) of a photograph which she lent, along with some of her other memorabilia, for an exhibition. The exhibition organizers returned her contributions piecemeal, and she recovered her precious photograph in a surprising way.

Miss Cooper's photograph

my mother always insisted I kept this stuff – I'd chains belonging to the march of the chainmakers – I've thrown some away because they got so rusty but I have kept one – they chained themselves together these chainmakers you see – anyhow – the – this when I went down to this 1968 reunion – I tell you – it was in Congress House – it was – you know – the Trade Union place and – it was very empty of the actual suffrage – there was a lot of Labour party stuff you see – but the actual suffrage stuff was missing you see – and – the – and oh they had voices – of Mrs Pankhurst and different – you know on gramophone records playing but mine occupied about a fifth and – that I took down and it was ages before I got it back because it was going up and down and all around the country getting a bit back and then a bit more back and there was one picture – of my mother in Hyde Park – speaking – with Mrs Fawcett – my mother didn't – Mrs Pankhurst stayed here but she got across with Mrs Pankhurst did my mother because –

most people did didn't they

yes well – anyhow she was speaking with Mrs Fawcett – she was the head of her suffrage society Mrs Fawcett – and – she – oh she was burning houses and she just lost her head – her and su-

Christabel

Christabel – well anyhow – where were – what was I telling you – let's think – what was where I'd got to

she was speaking with Mrs Fawcett in 1911

oh yes there was these voices coming on and – anyhow these had been passed all round England and I kept getting this lot back – the Labour Party had done it you see and they kept sending me another odd one back and there was such a lot missing – people were all keeping them – and I kept writing about it and finally there was just one picture missing – it – it was beautifully kept and it'd been taken about 1913 – perhaps in Hyde Park – and my mother speaking and Mrs Fawcett and different people on this platform and it didn't come back – and I kept asking her about it – I rang up – Betty Lockwood – you know – in London and – they couldn't they couldn't find it – well anyhow there was a do on television – on ITV – about suffrage movement and if that blooming picture wasn't on it – and I knew it was the only one – and it was from – Bristol – it was from West you know see and I knew it was the only one in existence – you see it was on and in the course of it this picture came on you

see and they'd all remarked that it was the only one like it – it was the platform
full and crowds of people all round it so I wrote to Betty Lockwood and told
her and I got it the following week – they'd borrowed it for the film you see

Some of this text is difficult to follow without context; for instance the
deictic references to 'this stuff'. Speakers normally share a physical setting,
so that references can meaningfully be made to objects present, but a writer
has to be careful to establish any references explicitly. Facial expressions and
gesture are an important part of the meaning in face-to-face speech. When
Miss Cooper refers to 'this stuff', she might point to it, take hold of it or
indicate it with a dismissive gesture. When she says 'Yes, well' in response to
the interviewer's comment on Mrs Fawcett, her facial expression might show
thoughtfulness, impatience or agreement. These features can be indicated in
writing, but they can not form part of the direct feedback between addresser
and addressee.

A speaker often requires constant reassurance that the hearer can follow
and understand, so feedback phrases such as 'you see' and 'you know' are
used to check that the hearer can identify a particular reference:

Betty Lockwood – you know – in London
it was from West you know see

They can also be used to signal explanations:

it was – you know – the Trade Union place
the Labour party had done it you see

Miss Cooper also uses them to point up significant moments in the narrative:

this picture came on you see

Spoken discourse and written texts are often organized differently. Written texts can be redrafted until they conform to conventional patterns of
organization, but once an utterance has been spoken, the speaker is more or
less committed to it. For example, when Miss Cooper starts talking about
Mrs Fawcett and Christabel burning houses she departs from the account of
the photograph, and has to call on the *speaker–hearer feedback* mechanism to
get herself back on track. Similarly, the fact that the picture was 'the only
one' is an important piece of background information, so it would normally
occur early in a written account. In her spoken discourse, Miss Cooper has
to add this fact after she has built her narrative to its climax – 'and if that
blooming picture wasn't on it...'. Then she has to create a second climax
using the additional significance of the photograph's uniqueness – 'you see it
was on and in the course of it this picture came on you see'. In this respect,
the repetition and redundancy which is such a characteristic of speech helps
to compensate for the fact that background details, explanations and inciden-
tal points have somehow to be integrated with the account of events. The
following, for instance, might look like simple redundancy:

(a) they had voices ... on gramophone records
   there was these voices coming on
(b) it was going up and down and all around the country
   these had been passed all round England
(c) I knew it was the only one
   it was the only one in existence
   it was the only one like it

In the case of (a) and (b), the repeated utterances allow Miss Cooper to take up the threads of her account after the diversion about Mrs Fawcett. The repetitions of (c) might be an attempt to make up for the lapse in not mentioning the picture's uniqueness earlier in the discourse. In formal written language such reiterations may be unnecessary because the writer can restructure the text as whole, and it is always possible for the reader to re-read it.

In exchange for the speaker's consideration for the hearer's problems in following spoken discourse, a hearer will normally make allowances for such features as false starts, – 'anyhow the – this – when I went down ...', difficulties in making references and identifications – 'her and su – ur/Christabel/ Christabel', and unfinished sentences and phrases – 'my mother didn't'.

As well as exploring this text through discussion, students can find it useful to present the information in different forms, for example as part of a chapter in Miss Cooper's biography or a paragraph for an official history of the suffragette movement. In the course of these activities students might focus on dialect forms, though this is likely to be done in the context of a host of other features to be edited out in the process of transforming the text into written Standard English. Some of the expressions which students might feel the need to formalize or replace include:

this stuff
they chained themselves together these chainmakers
it was very empty
it was going up and down and all round the country
she got across with Mrs Pankhurst did my mother
she was the head of her suffrage society Mrs Fawcett
I kept getting this lot back

In transforming the account into the written mode students will need to ensure that the text is in sentences. In Miss Cooper's spoken version the basic unit of planning is not the sentence but the clause, with clauses often related by 'and', or by an adjunct such as 'anyhow'.

Students might also note that Miss Cooper uses only one form for the past tense of 'to be' in some constructions:

there was a lot of Labour Party stuff
there was one picture

there was these voices ...
there was such a lot missing

These features all suggest a degree of informality in Miss Cooper's speech, indicating that she was probably comfortable with her surroundings, her audience and the events she was relating. It is important that students of language understand and appreciate this context of informality, and the corresponding features of language, as well as being able to identify and describe the syntactic patterns of phrases and sentences which have been abstracted from it. Language study built on a rich and intimate acquaintanceship with discourse can be generous, rigorous and positive. But students who are not given opportunities to understand where data comes from can only engage with language issues as a series of sterile puzzles. To avoid the opposite but twin traps of overformalization and untethered subjectivity, students need direct experience of relevant discourse as well as descriptive frameworks for understanding it.

The issue of what form such frameworks should take has been the subject of intense debate throughout the development of A Level English Language courses. In an account of the syllabus published in the NATE publication *Alternatives at English A Level* (NATE, 1988), Bill Greenwell makes the following observation:

> This syllabus grew out of proposals rejected by the JMB as lacking a sufficient body of knowledge. The revised 1981 proposals placed a greater emphasis upon the acquisition of theoretical, linguistic terminology.

In fact, this characterization of the syllabus's development covers a significant divergence of views about what kinds of response are expected from students. One view amounts to saying that the main aim of the language study aspect of the syllabus should be to ensure that students should master linguistic terminology. An alternative view is that students should have opportunities to develop their own theories, ideas, methods' for studying the topics given on the syllabus; that too little is known about how 17-year-olds can cope with the complex demands of studying language acquisition, sociolinguistics and discourse analysis to be able to specify in much detail or with too much confidence what they ought to know; and that teachers and examiners should have the freedom to set investigative tasks and examination questions in relation to what was actually being taught, as long as it fitted in with the general framework and aims of the syllabus. In a sense, the issue is how far it is possible to trust classroom teachers and their students to develop ways of exploring language without specifying from the top down what descriptive categories and explanatory theories should provide the basis of their thinking.

The practical consequence of this debate as far as the JMB's A Level English Language syllabus is concerned was that general guidance is given where it is considered relevant and useful for each section of Paper 1, but that the syllabus does not specify a metalanguage or theoretical frameworks.

Students of language certainly do need a terminology or metalanguage for discussing language. But the aim of language awareness and language study at this level is to develop the terminologies which students already have, however unsystematic, subjective and partial these may be, by engagement with language in use. In other words, students derive their 'terms' through the learning process itself, and since the direction of learning in so vast and complex a subject cannot be predicted, it is certainly vain, and may be counterproductive, to attempt to specify *a priori* what terms or concepts may be needed. No amount of metalanguage can substitute for students' direct and honest observations, and even a low-level subjective response which attempts to engage with a text on its own terms contains possibilities for further exploration, and is in that sense preferable to a mechanical feature-spotting strategy of the kind which could too easily be encouraged by superimposed linguistic categories and checklists of terms. Experience of teaching and assessment for the A Level English Language syllabus has shown that giving students the ability to identify examples of, for instance, *phonological patterning, alliteration, simile and metaphor, inflection, compound, collocation, co-ordination and subordination* does not of itself help them to understand, for example, the social consequences of using regional dialects, or how children's use of syntax develops, or how a promotional text achieves its purpose.

An example may clarify the kinds of learning opportunity which occur frequently on A Level English Language courses. The 1987 Paper 1 contained a question which required students to identify and describe some of the distinctive features of language of two from a choice of four passages. One passage consisted of an extract from one of Winston Churchill's wartime speeches and the question suggested that students should pay attention to such matters as vocabulary and meaning, grammar, structure as well as any other relevant linguistic matters.

JMB A Level English Language 1987 Paper 1

However matters go in France or with the French government, or another French government, we in this island and in the British Empire will never lose our sense of comradeship with the French people. If we are now called upon to endure what they have been suffering, we shall emulate their courage, and if final victory rewards our toils they shall share the gains, aye, and freedom shall be restored to all. We abate nothing of our just demands; not one jot or tittle do we recede. Czechs, Poles, Norwegians, Dutch, Belgians, have joined their causes to our own. All these shall be restored.

What General Weygand called the Battle of France is over. I expect that the Battle of Britain is about to begin. Upon this battle depends the survival of Christian civilization.

Upon it depends our own British life and the long continuity of our institutions and our Empire. The whole fury and might of the enemy must very soon be turned on us. Hitler knows that he will have to break us in this island or lose the war. If we can stand up to him all Europe may be free and the life of the world may move forward into broad sunlit uplands. But if we fail, then the whole world, including the United States, including all that we have known and cared for, will sink into the abyss of a new Dark Age made more sinister, and perhaps more protracted, by the lights of a perverted science.

Let us therefore brace ourselves to our duties, and so bear ourselves that if the British Empire and its Commonwealth last for a thousand years, men will still say 'This was their finest hour'.

(JMB, *English Language Advanced Paper 1*, Tuesday 19 May 1987)

One student's answer to this questions was as follows. (The paragraphs are numbered for reference.)

Candidate's answer to 1987 Paper 1, Section C Question 9

1 There are interesting linguistic devices employed here by Winston Churchill. One which is particularly striking is the way in which his sentences are structured so that the sentence ends with an upbuilding thought; 'if final victory rewards our toils [...] freedom shall be restored to all'. This is much more encouraging than 'Freedom shall be restored if final victory rewards our toils.'

2 By his compliments to the British he appeals to their patriotism and sense of pride – 'our Empire', 'British life' – and then tells them that they must go to war. Structure is all important to the meaning here, and the effect which it has is absolutely vital. The use of very powerful imagery to stir up emotion is employed, and the whole extract has the feel of a very skilful political speech. 'All that we know and care for' sink into a 'Dark Age' of 'perverted science'. Churchill is almost implying a divine approval by use of expressions such as 'survival of Christian civilization' and calls the Germans 'sinister'. Speeches such as this did nothing to conquer the problems of nationalism, instead it fuelled a hatred of anything not British. The conclusion of the speech leaves the hearers in a state which is highly emotional, and in which they would be ready to face the whole German army: men will say 'This was their finest hour'.

3 Churchill employed techniques used by salesmen and advertisers today. He appealed to the side of humans which envisioned themselves as heroes, and the side which saw a future of 'broad sunlit uplands'. If these people had been realistic, they would have seen that such a thing could never be possible after the devastation of the war, but Churchill employed the language here with all the skill of an evangelical preacher, building up and up towards an emotional peak in which the men of England would be psychologically ready for anything.

4 This passage shows how language can be used to stimulate different parts of the mind, in this case the emotional.

This answer shows a strong sense of the text's general purposes and of its degree of affective charge by discussing the likely effects on addressees, and by referring to the social and historical context. The genre, *political speech*, is accurately identified, and the intertextual references to 'salesmen' and 'advertisers' and to 'evangelical preachers' offer useful, if implicit, assimilations in terms of persuasive purposes and techniques. Climactic structures and ordering of clauses for effect are identified as rhetorical devices, but most of the analysis is done by means of common rather than technical stylistic frameworks of description, with references to 'compliments', 'appeals to', 'tells' [them], 'stir up' [emotion], 'implying' [approval], 'fuelled' [hatred].

Structurally, the answer falls into four parts, roughly identifiable with its four constituent paragraphs. Paragraph 1 identifies grammatical devices and persuasive effect, Paragraph 2 is the heart of the answer, with Paragraph 3 being nearly a reworking of Paragraph 2, perhaps an attempt to push Paragraph 2's issues further. Paragraph 4 is a general conclusion. It seems fair to assume that Paragraph 1 was in some ways a false start, so the main issue for the answer is how it could have developed the ideas in Paragraph 2 relevantly, given the limitations of time and exam pressure.

Observations in Paragraph 2 which are developed tend to use non-linguistic frameworks, history and psychology in particular, with some subjective judgements about the text's morality. The pattern is repeated in Paragraph 3, yet Paragraph 2 has plenty of possibilities for discussion which is more relevant to language use. For example, the student might have asked, and tried to answer, some of the following questions, each based on a phrase used in that paragraph:

● 'very powerful imagery'

What examples of this are represented in the text of the speech?
What are the images based on?
What makes them powerful?

● 'a skilful political speech'

How do we recognize the text as political, rather than, say, religious?
How do we identify it as the text of a speech rather than as a primarily written text?
What makes it skilful?

● 'implying divine approval'

How is the religious register expressed?
How does this point relate to the comparison with preaching in Paragraph 3?

● 'a state which is highly emotional'

What emotive or evocative terms are used?
How are they distributed in the text?

Development of these points, which constitute the main linguistic ideas of the answer's Paragraph 2, would, on the evidence of the answer's general level of response, seem to be well within the capabilities of the student. They match the criterion of relevance to the question, being related to characteristics which contribute to our recognition of the distinctive kind of text it is in terms of genre, purpose and style. They are clearly relevant to the text itself, while raising wider issues about language use. And they take language as their focus rather than psychology, history or morality. The only technical items needed to help this student develop a descriptive framework were *register* and *emotive*, and very often it is just such general terms which prove the most useful in allowing students to differentiate and order their own responses.

While the syllabus does consist of four more or less equally weighted components, it is the balance between them which constitutes the spirit and aim of the syllabus: 'to combine learning about the nature and functions of language ... with learning how to use English more effectively'.

Quite complex relationships between the four syllabus components have been established, in principle by the structure of the syllabus, and in practice by the way the syllabus has been implemented by school and college English departments. For example, 'intellectual understanding ... about language', specified as one of the objectives of the examination, is assessed explicitly by Paper 1, the Project and the commentary on Original Writing, but also implicitly by the analytical skills required by the interpretation and comprehension of texts for Paper 2. The key parameters of *purpose* and *audience* and the investigative spirit of the syllabus apply to all four syllabus components in different and complementary ways.

The first of the two overarching aims of the syllabus, 'intellectual understanding ... about language and its uses', is being achieved thanks to the energy and adaptability of teachers, though many teachers, and particularly those from centres new to the syllabus, express a need for considerable inservice training on language study, particularly in the first two or three years. Once securely established, however, its place on an advanced scheme of work for language study and language skills is generally recognized.

An informal survey conducted by questionnaire in 1990 showed that centres, mainly sixth form colleges and Further Education colleges but including a few 11–18 schools, were responding very positively to A Level English Language. Students were described as enthusiastic, though some regarded it as just another A Level. There was considerable feedback from students who had moved into Higher Education and employment on how useful the course had been to them. Many centres described the benefit to students of task-based learning, and the high level of motivation resulting from the variety of approaches within the syllabus as well as the opportunities for initiative in individual research and work with the spoken word as well as writing.

One centre particularly valued the course's emphasis on purposeful writing for a specific purpose and audience, the self-motivation developed by coursework, self-awareness learnt in the process of writing commentaries and the editing skills used in Paper 2. The Original Writing component often provided the initial attraction, with students gradually coming to terms with more challenging aspects, such as case studies and language theory, and learning to cope with the inevitable workload of coursework.

Some centres found some aspects of the syllabus more difficult than others. One centre summed up a widespread view in stating that literature-trained teachers tend to be wary of language theory, that stylistics can be difficult to teach, but that the Project is particularly valuable educationally. Another centre spoke of the drudgery of coursework administration and some initial uncertainties about where to pitch theory. However, others welcomed opportunities offered by the syllabus to develop expertise and confidence in new areas, and there was general recognition of the value of new approaches to cultural awareness through explorations of the roots of language and the study of discourse.

The practical worries of centres new to the syllabus included some concern that recruitment for A Level English Literature classes would be adversely affected. In some cases literature numbers declined for some years, then increased again, with total intake eventually doubling or trebling. Most claimed that literature was largely unaffected, and some said that a renewed interest in 'English' had increased literature numbers. The general impression that, as one centre pointed out, the course mainly recruits from students who would not have been attracted to English Literature A Level seems to be confirmed by the finding that A Level English Language combines successfully with the whole range of other A Level subjects, including mathematics, social sciences and 'hard' sciences as well as modern languages and other arts and humanities subjects.

The problems and difficulties most often referred to were time management, especially for coursework consultation and preparation, difficulties in organizing courses to ensure a fair balance between coursework and exam preparation, some insecurity on the part of colleagues about teaching case studies and language theory, particularly what were perceived to be the more technical areas of language acquisition, language change and stylistics. There was general agreement that resources were in short supply, particularly appropriate textbooks, with a consequent strain on photocopying budgets. Some centres also mentioned that some teachers tended to underestimate the radical aims of the syllabus, and another, acknowledging the coherence of the syllabus as its greatest strength, commented on the difficulties of relating the language theory to aspects of students' own writing and research.

There was general agreement among the 11–18 schools that knowledge and expertise developed by the A Level teachers contributed to their confidence in developing Knowledge About Language with 11–16 pupils. Work on case studies at A Level had helped departments to reassess approaches to writing at 11–16, with more emphasis on audience, form and function and on writing for real purposes.

6 Relating language study and language experience at 16+

The principle that the more formal aspects of language should emerge from pupils' and students' intuitive concerns with the social and human context of texts and discourses applies to all the language theory areas of A Level English language as well as to language awareness in the earlier secondary years. Translating this principle into classroom practice means encouraging a generously wide definition of language study consistent with some of the intuitive strategies students adopt to come to terms with challenging issues. For example, the following passage is an extract from a letter written by the wife of Sir John Pelham to her husband in his absence on a campaign during the later part of the reign of Richard II (1377–1399). It appeared on Paper 1 of JMB A Level English Language in 1987, with the instruction to describe and comment on some of the changes which had taken place in English spelling, vocabulary and grammar since it was written, and I used it as a starting point for discussing historical varieties of English with a Year 12 class.

My dere Lord, I recommande me to your hie Lordeschipp wyth hert & body, & all my pore myght; and wyth all this I think zow, as my dere Lorde, derest & best yloved of all erthlyche Lordes; I say for me, and thanke yhow, my dere Lord, with all thys that I say before, off your comfortable lettre that ze send me from Pownefraite that com to me on Mary Magdaleyn day; ffor by my trowth I was never so gladd as when I herd by your lettre that ye warr stronge ynogh, wyth the grace off God, for to kepe you fro the malyce of your ennemys ... And my dere Lord iff it lyk zow for to know off my ffare, I am here by layd in manner off a sege, with the counte of Sussex, Sudray, & a great parcyll off Kente, so that I ne may noght out nor none vitayles gette me, bot wt myche hard. Wharfore my dere iff it lyk zow, by the awyse off zowr wyse counsell, for to sett remedye off the salvation off yhower Castell, and wtstand the malyce off thes schires forsayde. And also that ye be fullyche enformed off these grett malce wyrkers in these schyres whych yt haffes so dispytffully wrogth to zow, and to zowr castell, to yhowr men, and to zour tenants, ffore this cuntree have yai wastede, for a gret whyle. Farewele my dere Lorde; the Holy Trinyte zow kepe fro zour ennemys, and son send me gud tythings off yhow.

Ywrten at Pevensay in the castel on Saynt Jacobe day last past,

By yhowr awnn pore

J. Pelham

My teaching agenda corresponded to the terms of the examination question's concern with English spelling, vocabulary and grammar, and accordingly treated the text as data for observations and analysis. My focus therefore concerned such issues as:

- *Spelling*
  How is the use of 'y' and 'i' different from twentieth century English spelling, e.g. 'wyth', 'myght', 'earthlyche', 'thys'?
  Compare the use of 'f' and 'ff' in fourteenth and twentieth century English writing, e.g. 'ffor', 'off', 'iff', 'dispytffully'.
- *Lexis*
  How have these words changed in meaning and usage since the fourteenth century – 'malyce', 'parcyll', 'vitayles', 'wastede'?
- *Grammar*
  How would you describe the differences between fourteenth and twentieth century English as shown in the grammatical structures of these sentences and phrases?

I recommande me ...	*Focus*: reflexives
I herd by your lettre ...	*Focus*: prepositions
for to kepe you ... for to know ... for to sett remedye	*Focus*: non-finite verb marking
if it lyk zow	*Focus*: subject–verb–object
I ne may noght out nor none vitayles gette me	*Focus*: negation
that ze send me ... that com to me	*Focus*: verb tense

After some attempts to find ways of talking about these issues, my students' alternative agenda began to emerge. What caught their attention was the plight of the writer. Some recalled a project from their Year 7 English lessons entitled *School Under Siege* in which they had to imagine that the whole school was quarantined for three weeks, and they had each written a 'Letter Home'. Otherwise, there was little within their own direct experience to which they could assimilate the experience of a siege. Yet they were intrigued by the possibilities of the situation. They wondered how a letter could have been delivered from a besieged castle, how Lord Pelham's 'comfortable lettre' was able to find its way through the siege, how those besieged managed to get supplies, and what Lady Pelham meant by 'wt myche hard'. They speculated that letters would have been more important in the fourteenth century than they are in the twentieth, and how receiving a letter, which had perhaps been carried through difficult and dangerous circumstances, would be very much a special occasion.

Their consideration of the weight and significance of this letter led them to wonder at Lady Pelham's tone; was the ingratiating tone of the first part sincere or conventional? Or was it part of her strategy to get her husband to help her, a 'defenceless female' act? They were not sure whether 'iff it lyk zow for to know off my ffare' was sarcastic, and they were puzzled by what the relationship between Lady Pelham and her husband must have been like. They found it unthinkable that a twentieth century European woman would heap compliments like this without irony.

These contextual and social considerations helped the students to take care in interpreting some of the key phrases and sentences, and they began to focus on aspects of the letter which are problematic linguistically as well as historically. For example,

- 'your comfortable lettre'

  Does 'comfortable' just mean 'comforting', or is Lady Pelham trying to suggest that her husband is in a comfortable situation while she is suffering?

- 'iff it lyk zow for to know off my ffare'

  What would be the nearest modern English equivalent to this phrase? Might it be 'If you really want to know ...' [sarcastic], or 'Let me tell you how I am getting on ...'. And why does she write 'If it lyk zow' rather than 'If you like?'

- 'I ne may noght out nor none vitayles gette me, bot wt myche hard'

  Does Lady Pelham mean that she can't get out of the castle at all, or just that this is very difficult? Were the multiple negatives 'ne ... noght ... nor none' normal in the English language at this time, or was Lady Pelham trying to emphasize her difficulties?

The students began to notice patterns of usage: the religious references – 'all erthlyche Lordes', 'Mary Magdaleyn day', 'wyth the grace of God', 'the Holy Trinyte zow kepe', 'Saynt Jacobe day', and the use of three different spellings of 'your' in the structure 'to zowr castell', 'to yhowr men', 'and to zour tenants'. Their problems with the term 'comfortable' led them to notice that other words were out of focus with modern usage. For example:

the 'malyce' of your ennemys
the 'counte' of Sussex

a great 'parcyll' off Kente
'vitayles'
the 'salvation' off yhower Castell

And so by degrees they concentrated on the more formal aspects of the text, and began to use it as data for thinking about some of the ways in which language, and the social relations and institutions which breathe life and meaning into it, had changed during the past 500 years. Only by securing a framework for the writer's role, the audience, the text's purposes and the social context were the students able to focus onto the more narrowly linguistic aspects of the text.

A great deal of the text-based discussion and exploration in A Level English courses is devoted to exploring these fundamental concepts, none of which is as simple as many students first assume. How, for example, is a text's readership to be defined? Extrinsic factors, such as age, social class and occupation may be important, but many texts address themselves to reader's interests, values and cultural assumptions. Purposes are not always obvious; a text which purports to inform may also have a persuasive subtext. Students may derive their models for these concepts from limited genres, such as advertising, where 'audience = market', and the social context is stereotyped as economics and social prestige, so engagement with a wide variety of texts may be necessary to help students build and revise their understanding. In this sense, an A Level student attempting to relate the tone, lexis and grammar of an article or review to her perception of the kind of person who might read it, to work out what the text is trying to do, and which words and phrases are carrying the weight of its purposes, and to probe the ideologies and values through which the text speaks, is, in the adult sense of the activity, learning to read.

This fragile and complex process requires an extended illustration. The texts for discussion and comment appeared in Section C of the 1989 A Level English Language paper, and the written response is one student's answer. The full question, texts and answer are as follows;

Question 8 from A Level English Language Section C Paper 1 1989

8   The first of the two passages which follow is from a journal published by the United Nations Association called *New World* (1983). It is read mainly by people interested in international relations and political and humanitarian issues. The second is from *Aircraft Illustrated* (1986), a journal read mainly by people of all ages who are interested in civil and military aircraft.

Compare some of the ways in which language is used in these two articles to achieve their purposes.

In your answer, you should refer to vocabulary and meanings, grammar, overall structure and any other linguistic matters you think are relevant.

Passage A

Call for a ban on 'war' toys

The European Parliament wants the production and sale of 'war' toys reduced and replaced by toys which are 'constructive and develop creativity'.

Last year they passed a resolution calling on member states to ban the 'visual and verbal advertising of war toys' and Sweden, France and the Federal Republic of Germany, the world's third largest toy producer, have moved towards ultimately pegging the production of war toys.

A substantial number of individuals and organisations in the United Kingdom have expressed concern about the present state of affairs.

The European Parliament's resolution recommended in particular that the sale of replica guns and rifles which are so realistic that they might be mistaken for the real thing should be banned in order to avoid them being used by criminals.

It emphasised the danger of giving children, through war toys, a liking for weapons and expressed concern at the part the mass media was playing in 'creating a culture of war and violence'.

The resolution believed that if the production of war toys was reduced there would be a demand for other toys – particularly electronic toys and musical instruments – and asked that help should be given to manufacturers who had to install expensive new equipment and technology to make the switch.

Passage B

Revised Phantom

Matchbox's kit of the Spey-powered Phantom FG1/FGR2 has now been revised to bring the model up to the latest standard, and to improve some less desirable features.

In shape, the model was reasonably accurate, except for the front end. The original model had a radome that was too small in diameter, but this has now been changed by the adoption of a larger radome and the lower line of the front fuselage has also been revised. The electronic-countermeasures bar, a unique feature of RAF Phantoms, has now been added.

Matchbox's kit of the Spey-Phantom has a comprehensive weapons and stores fit. In the pure interceptor role the model has the four Sparrows (or Skyflashes) and four Sidewinders, with a vulcan gun pod or long-range tank under the fuselage. Long-range tanks may be carried on integral pylons on the outer wing positions. In the strike role, bombs or rocket pods can be fitted, again with the Vulcan gun pod. A reconnaissance pod for mounting under the fuselage is also included. Of course, a mix of all these weapons, pods and tanks can be selected as required for a particular subject.

A unique feature of the Royal Navy's F-4K Phantom FG1 was the extending nose wheel strut to give a higher angle of attack for catapult launching, and the kit includes both the normal length nose undercarriage unit and the unit in the extended position.

Markings are supplied for three Spey-Phantoms. One is an FG1 from No 111 Squadron based at RAF Leuchars, Scotland, in 1983. The second is an

FG1 of No 892 Squadron, RN Fleet Air Arm, based on HMS *Ark Royal*, during 1977. The last subject is an FGR2 of No 23 Squadron based at RAF Stanley, in the Falkland Isles, during 1983.

This is a useful revision of the only available Spey-Phantom kit in 1:72 scale.

The cost is £3.95.

This student's response to these texts was as follows:

Candidate's answer to Question 8

Passage A's purpose is to inform people about the discussion on 'war toys' and show how such things can be potentially dangerous. However, Passage B is waging no moral crusade and is informing us, being more of an advertisement for the kit. These differences in purpose are related to the people who read the magazine. Passage A's writer knows his 'humanitarian' readership will want to know what the moral issues are, whereas Passage B's writer actually is trying to sell what Passage A's is trying to ban. His readership is concerned with aircraft not humanitarian issues.

Passage A's writer uses direct quotes from the European parliament to show the senselessness of 'war' toys. He mentions that different countries are against them and then says that 'individuals' and 'organisations' in the UK also want to ban them. This use of proper and collective nouns is trying to show that most people are against the 'toys'. This article has few technical terms within it because it is aimed at a wide readership. Passage B is aimed at a specific readership, aircraft enthusiasts, so it includes technical words like 'radome' and 'electronic-countermeasures'. It assumes that its readership has the knowledge to understand these terms.

Both articles use lists to achieve their purposes. As has been mentioned, Passage A uses lists to show the support against the war toys. Passage B lists the features of an individual war toy to show the reader that it is an accurate model. The third paragraph of Passage B lists the 'missiles', 'gun pods' and 'weapons' of the Phantom. So Passage A's writer is using a list technique to emphasise that 'war toys' are wrong, whereas Passage B's writer is trying to sell the toys.

The realism of the war toys is why Passage A's writer wants the toys banned. But Passage B's writer is using this realism as a selling point. The Matchbox Phantom is an extremely worthwhile purchase because of its many features. Passage A has few adjectives and those that there are are factual, like 'substantial'. This is because its purpose is to inform. However, Passage B has several adjectives and these are mainly emotive, like 'desirable', 'latest', 'accurate' and 'comprehensive'. This is because its purpose is to persuade the reader to buy the model.

Passage A talks generally about 'war toys' because the writer wants them all banned, and his readership do not need to know the specific types. Passage B talks specifically about the Phantom. He is not making a general statement.

Both articles are aimed mainly at an adult readership. Passage A deals with concepts like 'creativity' and 'culture' which a young person would find hard to understand. Passage B uses technical terms which a child would not understand. This suggests that Passage A's assumption about the war toys affecting young children is wrong. In fact, from the language in Passage B, it seems as though the toys are for adults not the young.

Both articles use repetition. Passage A repeats words like 'culture' and 'concern', whereas in Passage B words like 'pods' and 'weapons' are repeated. The repetition in Passage A draws a contrast between the 'evil' toys and shows what the writer wants adults and children to possess. They are abstract ideas associated with morality. The repetition in Passage B is merely to emphasise the vast array of features the Phantom possesses. They are actual items because the writer is trying to sell you the toy not awaken your conscience.

Passage A has within it negative vocabulary to show the bad side of 'war toys', like 'criminals'. However, Passage B is full of positive, persuasive vocabulary, like 'useful' and 'unique' in order to persuade the reader that the Phantom is worth buying.

This student's answer uses contrasts in purposes between the two texts to draw inferences about audience. Readership is defined initially in terms of interests, though later in the answer age group is discussed as a defining criterion, and these observations are related to the lexis of the texts. The answer gives a brief paraphrase of Passage A, with comment to indicate how contrasts in the uses of lexical items relate to the nature of the texts' readers. The answer mentions various different purposes of lists, the issue of 'realism', emotive lexis, persuasion, repetition, and contrasts between 'positive' and 'negative' lexis.

Two main purposes for Passage A are identified ('to inform' and 'to show') and two main purposes for Passage B (to inform and to promote – suggested by the phrase 'trying to sell'). The answer shows some understanding of the idea that one kind of language function can be used to realize another, suggesting for example that the task of persuading need not be emotive, but may be achieved simply through the expression of information – 'Passage B is waging no moral crusade and is informing us, being more of an advertisement for the kit.'

The seemingly obvious concept of *audience* turns out in practice to be quite subtle. In this answer, the student recognizes that the salient characteristics of an 'audience' relate to attitudes, interests and beliefs, and that texts are written to these aspects. The key terms are 'humanitarian' and 'aircraft enthusiasts', though the answer never fully brings out the implied contrast between the issues about which each readership chooses to be informed.

As a general exploration of the concepts of audience and purpose the answer has some useful directions for further comment, and some implications for teaching and language development. But its comments on the language bring the answer up against the limitations of its own framework for describing textual purposes. For example, in the fourth paragraph the answer relates the purposes of the passages to the frequency of occurrence of adjectives, especially emotive adjectives, claiming that 'Passage A has few adjectives … Passage B has several adjectives', justifying this view by citing the persuasive purpose of Passage B. In fact, the adjectives from Passage B quoted in the answer all have counterparts in Passage A:

Passage B	Passage A
desirable	constructive
latest	new
accurate	realistic
comprehensive	substantial

The answer has overselected data from the text to match an oversimplified expectation about how informative and persuasive functions are realized in texts. If anything, it is Passage A which is the more overtly persuasive, with its call for bans, its recommendations, emphasis on moral and cultural dangers and its enthusiasm for peaceful toys, thinly disguised as a report of official proceedings. Yet the student does have a point, picked up later in the answer in the assertion that Passage B 'is trying to sell you the toy not awaken your conscience', in that the amoral concern for technological detail makes it possible for the text to refer without conscious irony to the aircraft's 'less desirable features'.

There is evidence from the development of A Level English Language that such tentative insights, appropriately fostered and supported by varied and critical reading experience, and within the framework of a forum in which teachers and learners can respond to and evaluate texts, spoken and written, literary and otherwise, can enrich students' whole language experience, including their own productive development. But the quality of learning depends crucially on the development of shared terms of reference, assumptions and purposes; a shared language in the full sense.

The traditional forum for language development has been constituted by marginal and end-of-text written comments by the teacher, and also more recently by discussions between student and teacher for drafting, assessment and Records of Achievement. An important innovation for A Level English Language has been the creation of opportunities for students to apply ideas and techniques learnt in the area of language theory to their own original writing. The JMB's A Level English Language syllabus requires three pieces of original writing of different kinds as part of its coursework component, and the *Instructions and Guidance for Teachers* insists that 'Candidates will be expected to have undertaken a critical evaluation of their own writing and this should be incorporated into a commentary supplied with the pieces of writing along with any earlier drafts.' The guidance is elaborated as follows:

Commentaries

The purpose of the commentary must be to inform about the process of writing in all its aspects, including decisions made and alternatives chosen at a variety of levels.

The following guidelines may be useful:

- Factual information about origins, sources, adaptations, procedure, prior discussions etc. should accompany pieces as appropriate.
- Comments made about deletions, omissions, additions, revisions etc. with reference to earlier drafts are most useful.
- Accounts of audience responses (where appropriate) should be included especially where they have prompted revision or provoked justification.
- Observations on features of language (e.g. habitual phrases or sentence patterns) are much better than vague criticisms of general inadequacy.
- Reflections on problems encountered or on a student's writing development over the course are helpful.
- Description of differences between the three pieces submitted would provide a good opportunity for reflection upon style, register or other variation in written English.
- Comparison of a student's own writing with another student's or with an admired/tested model would be interesting.
- The amount of commentary necessary might depend on the type of original writing concerned.
- Sometimes an overall commentary on the three pieces of original writing would be more appropriate than critical evaluation/reflection on each.
- It might in some cases be appropriate to reward particularly good commentary writing with a mark allocation of up to 20 out of 50.

The commentary is an obligatory element of coursework at this level, and builds on good practice, including that established by GCSE coursework methods. It offers a space in which students can explore the complex relationship between language use and language theory in the context of their own writing, and their own theoretical frameworks about language. I would like to consider extracts from two commentaries written by students on A Level English Language courses, together with an indication of the pieces of original writing to which they refer.

The first extract consists of the opening four sections of a piece written to fulfil the requirements for an informative text.

LOCK UP YOUR HOME AND LOCK OUT CRIME

Your home is your castle ... but do you defend it?

There are more than 900,000 burglaries in Britain each year. That is one out of every 25 homes.

It does not matter where you live or what type of house you have, a burglary can be the most shattering experience of a life-time. It is hard to imagine just how unpleasant a burglary is, when a complete stranger breaks into YOUR home, rummages through YOUR things and helps himself to YOUR valued possessions, it's not just the expense that hurts, it's the distress that is caused, and the memories stolen for which no amount of insurance can compensate.

'It'll never happen to me.'

The FACT is that it may happen to you, so you should do something about it NOW, before you become just another burglary statistic. You don't have to live in a fortress to deter thieves. You just have to take a few precautions.

Most break-ins are the work of casual thieves on the look-out for an easy touch ... an empty house, an unlocked window, a door without a proper dead-lock. These are open invitations to a thief ... an invitation he'll find hard to resist.

'I thought I had nothing worth stealing.'

That is what many people say after a burglary, but by then they know that they were wrong.

In most cases, a burglar does not know exactly what he's going to find until he's inside your home. Once he's inside he will find something that will make the risk he's taking worthwhile.

It may be money, jewellery, TV's, videos, computers, cameras or antiques. Even the contents of a freezer are worth something to a thief.

All you have to do is look around your home at your valued possessions, and the chances are that a thief would value them too.

Is your home at risk?

It is true that some homes are more at risk than others from burglary. Flats and houses in Inner City areas often have a greater risk of burglary. If no-one is in your house all day and you are not overlooked, you are at greater risk – the majority of burglaries take place during the day, not at night as most people think.

Detached houses are also more at risk than semi-detached or terraced houses. This is because they are usually more secluded, and so neighbours cannot see the burglar.

Houses or flats at the ends of streets or backing into alleyways, parks, fields or waste ground are particularly at risk because of easy access. Walls, fences and shrubs around the garden may give you more privacy, but they also enable a burglar to get in unnoticed. Patio doors also give greater ease of entry into your home.

The important thing is that you are aware of the risks and do something about them. You do that by LOCKING UP YOUR HOME.

Before looking at extracts from the student's own commentary, it is worth identifying some of its more noticeable features in the terms suggested by the JMB's *Instructions and Guidance for Teachers*. The origins of this student's text clearly relate to the genre of mailshots designed to capitalize on home occupier's anxieties, and some of the more esoteric pieces of information, such as the point about the contents of a freezer, the fact that most burglaries take place during the day and the vulnerability of patio doors, clearly derive quite directly from these. The style is impersonal, though of a kind which will always have social and economic utility. The purpose may be characterizable as 'informational', but its primary function is clearly to soften up potential customers before revealing to them what practical steps they can take to lessen their anxieties, and at what price.

We learn how to write for a variety of purposes partly by imitating and using models, but an inadequate understanding of the nature of the chosen model seriously reduces the learning value of this activity. We sense that if this student has developed a reasonably detached view of the kind of text represented here, including perhaps a healthy scepticism for its ideological subtext, there is a chance that she may have moved her own writing development forwards. Otherwise she may simply have fulfilled a syllabus requirement and have no wider grasp of the creative possibilities in language.

The opening of her commentary runs as follows:

Extracts from student's commentary on 'Lock up your home'

I wanted to write an informative piece, but first I had to decide on a subject. I considered it best to write about a subject of which I was knowledgeable. Therefore I chose 'Crime Prevention', because at that time, a Home Watch scheme was being set up in my area, and I had read all the leaflets that had been distributed. However, I found that there was no booklet which gave a comprehensive account of all the aspects of crime prevention; each separate aspect was in a separate pamphlet.

Thus I decided to write a comprehensive booklet, containing all the factors I felt were relevant to protect against burglary. The audience for my piece would be home owners who were interested in improving the security of their house. I also decided to include some general hints about safety and crime prevention, e.g. property marking, Neighbourhood Watch, strangers at the door, etc.

I decided to present my writing in a booklet form. To attract the audience into picking up the booklet, I gave it an attractive cover. I decided that a catch-phrase on the cover would also serve to attract a reader, but it must also give a clue to what the booklet is going to be about. I decided that the phrase, 'Lock up your home ... and lock out crime' suited this purpose. I also drew a picture of a burglar entering a house, to show what could happen if you do not 'lock up your home'.

Once the reader has the booklet, it must be easy for him to read. I knew that as an informative piece, the information should be presented in a clear and concise manner. So I broke the writing into sections, so that it was easier to read. The headings that I gave to each section were to give an idea of what was to follow in that section. I used a variety of linguistic techniques. For example, rhetorical questions, 'Is your home at risk?' to make the reader ask himself whether he needs to do something; quotations and clichés, 'It'll never happen to me', 'I thought I had nothing worth stealing'. These are in an attempt to make the writing more personal, and therefore more influential on the reader, and also to show the popular misconceptions. I also used simple one-word headings which show simply what is to follow, e.g. 'windows', 'doors'.

When writing the text of the booklet, I decided that some kind of introduction was needed to inform the reader about the problems of burglary and to try and persuade the reader of the need for security. I achieved this by the use of facts and figures, e.g. 'There are more than 900,000 burglaries in Britain each year', and information of what a thief is looking for and what types of homes are more at risk.

Due to the nature of the piece, this introduction is also slightly persuasive in tone, i.e. I was trying to make the reader aware of the problem, but also convince him that he must do something about it. Thus I tried to appeal to the emotions with such sentences as 'a burglary can be the most shattering experience of a life-time' and 'It's not just the expense that hurts, it's the distress that is caused, and the memories stolen for which no amount of insurance can compensate.' I also hoped to achieve the same persuasive effects in the first section by placing the word 'YOUR' in capital letters. This emphasises that it may happen to you, and therefore made this information have more impact on the reader.

Another technique that I used, to make the writing more personal to the reader was the frequent use of ellipsis, e.g. it's, he's, don't, can't. This was an attempt to establish a more informal tone and a rapport with the reader.

At the end of the introductory section ... there is a reference to 'locking up your home'. This is written in capitals to give it emphasis. It also links back to the title of the booklet and the purpose of the booklet. This thought is, therefore, the most predominant in the reader's mind when he is reading the practical detailed information which follows about how to fit window locks and door locks.

This commentary recalls the aspect of the A Level English syllabus which requires students to 'respond critically to ... non-literary material'. This involves students in using their ideas about language to explore the language of a wide range of texts, spoken and written. When this process works as it should, students can develop their own frameworks for detached appraisal of their own writing and speech. In practice much can go wrong. Some students have understandable difficulty in separating language use from text content. Others simply stick rigidly to a predetermined descriptive framework, and apply it whether it is appropriate or not. Interpretation of syllabus divisions can discourage students from applying ideas and techniques learnt in one area of the syllabus to other areas. The range of genres and text types available for analysis and for using as the basis of original writing is simply so wide that the possibilities for direct overlap may be limited.

If anything, this student has overassimilated the lessons of discourse and text analysis and treated her own writing as if it were someone else's completed text rather than a stage, albeit a final one, in a constructive process of her own. Her account of the 'linguistic techniques' she uses – 'rhetorical questions ... quotations ... clichés' – looks like *post hoc* justification. Her easy acquiescence to the importance of surface features – 'an attractive cover ... a catch-phrase ... sections ... headings' – seems calculating. Her sense of the audience as already specified – 'home owners who were interested in improving the security of their house' – suggests that she did not take into account the role of the text itself in creating its audience by activating anxieties. Her acknowledgement of the need to compensate for the text's impersonality by bolting on 'appeal to the emotions', together with the 'attempts to make the writing more personal' and the addition of contractions – 'it's ... he's ... don't ... can't' – to try to create the effect of an informal tone in a text which is fundamentally otherwise, appears manipulative.

This student's commentary may well represent a use of knowledge about language of the kind which assumes a causal relationship between knowledge and competence. The student's references to drafting processes certainly suggest a very simple model. She casts about, not for a subject which matters to her, but for a topic with which to fulfil a preconceived purpose and specification, 'an informative piece' on 'a subject of which I was knowledgeable'. In each situation where a decision about style or content is required, the complex process of weighing up factors is reduced to 'I chose ...' or 'I decided ...'. The text is permeated with simple assumptions about causalities: A catch phrase and a picture 'attract' the reader; breaking the writing into sections makes the text easier to read; facts and figures persuade the reader of the need for security; certain linguistic techniques make information have more impact on the reader. We might conclude that if there is any causality in the relationship between this student's knowledge about language and her text, it is rather that the derivative and programmatic nature of her text 'causes' a dishonest commentary.

The forum in which students and their teachers can talk about texts stands on the ground of assumptions about language shared by both, and insofar as these are misconceived or limited, so the debates and negotiations which take place under their aegis will be distorted. But a framework of ideas about language which does justice to the place of the author in a text, the idea of audience and the complexities of textual purposes, as well as allowing honest exploration of themes and issues in written texts on their own terms, can offer powerful support to emerging writers. The following text and commentary from an A Level English Language student offers a more detailed record of the thinking that resulted in a final draft, including issues related to *purpose, audience, point of view, choice of vocabulary, structure,* and *tone.*

What on earth are you doing?

THE EARTH IS DYING. It has a cancer festering and growing by the day. If it is not cured it threatens to slowly eradicate every life form in the sea, air and on the land. What is this threat?

It is YOU and the rest of your parasitical race.

Yes, you and the rest of your species have abused and raped planet earth since you first set foot on her surface.

The Romans stripped trees from the once lush shores of the southern Mediterranean to make room for fields. The top soil eroded and the shores became desert; a state in which you still find them today, over 2000 years later. But that did not teach you as the dustbowls of the central USA and the rapid advance of the Sahara desert testify.

You could halt the process and perhaps even reverse it. But you are only interested in fattening your already corpulent bodies and wallets still further and not in the survival of your children.

IN THE PAST 100 YEARS YOUR ASSAULTS HAVE GROWN WORSE: THE CONSEQUENCES GREATER AND THE CHANCES OF REDEMPTION LESS.

You choose not to see that the clouds of smoke which your factories vomit into the atmosphere remain there as a shroud around the earth. This is causing global temperatures to rise, because the heat from the sun does not dissipate. These rises may only be a few degrees, but already they are having a major effect on the climate and weather systems throughout the planet. Witness the recent heat wave in Greece. Imagine your children having to suffer such conditions only ten times worse.

You just cannot see that if you continue your pogrom of the rainforests, at current rates, there will soon be very little of these priceless jewels left and that countless numbers of unique species will have been obliterated. That aside, the rainforests are the earth's oxygen generators, and without their photosynthesis you are condemning your offspring to slow suffocation. Just because you want quick returns on your timber.

Some of the poisons you pump into your atmosphere do come back. Mixed with rainwater, they produce the all too familiar acid rain, which has devastated European and British lakes and forests. Yes that is Britain, your 'Oh so great' nation. This is no longer some other government's problem, it affects all nations.

POLLUTION RECOGNISES NO FRONTIERS

Your generation really does not care. You are content to live your lives bleeding and poisoning the planet and to leave the legacy of destruction and irreversible disaster to your children.

You really cannot continue this voracious pillage of your own home.

The planet is crying out for you to ask the question

WHAT ON EARTH
ARE WE DOING?

Before your children have to ask:

WHAT IN HELL
DID THEY DO?

> If you want to act now join
> ### GREEN EARTH
> I wish to donate
>
> ☐ £5 ☐ £10 ☐ Other (specify) _____
>
> Signed..
>
> To receive your newsletter send a
> cheque or p.o. along with your
> address to:
> ### GREEN EARTH
> Manchester
> M2

As with *Lock Up Your Home*, this text, *What On Earth* ...? is derivative though in this case the author has made the text her own, particularly through the direct and accusing address to the reader, and also in the passionate tone and the general tendency to personify aspects of the environment. Choice of mature adults as the paradigm readership also makes it permissible for the student to experiment with the effects of lexical items which it may otherwise be difficult for a 17-year-old to use unselfconsciously – 'parasitical', 'corpulent', 'pogrom', 'voracious'.

The tendency to overstate is a general feature of the persuasive writing of young people, particularly when the issue is one to which they feel committed. In this case, we might wonder whether such very strong terms as 'cancer', 'raped', 'pogrom', 'devastated', 'disaster' have been earned by factual support. We might observe the sleight of hand which shifts from 'you and your parasitical race' to 'Your generation', but acknowledge that, while some of the text's content comes across as ingenuous, its challenge is impossible to evade. Among other things, we want to know how deliberately we are being manipulated and how personally we should take the accusations. The author's commentary might offer us the key to these questions.

Extracts from student's commentary on 'What on earth are you doing?'

The final draft of this piece was presented as a leaflet, aimed to persuade a middle aged audience to, at the very least, treat their environment with more respect but primarily to join or donate money to a 'Green' party. However, the first draft was very different from the third presentation, and many alterations were made in the production process.

First draft

This was a very short piece of around one hundred and fifty words. Although I felt it was fairly hard-hitting, I also realised that it was very general, and some of the impact was lost because it had no specific audience to deliver its message to.

The style and structure were poem-like, with an introductory paragraph, followed by four paragraphs which criticise the human race, and finally there was a question designed to leave the reader considering what they have just read.

I felt that the vocabulary used throughout was not hard-hitting enough. I was trying to stir people's emotions, and I felt that such words as 'alter', 'upset' and 'tamper' were not sufficiently hard-hitting. Their effect could perhaps have been strengthened by adding an adverb, for example, 'radically alter', 'totally upset'. However, this may have detracted from the succinctness of the piece.

Second draft

This was drastically different from the first draft. It was longer but had a narrower subject in that I decided to concentrate entirely on the abuse of the environment, excluding nuclear weapons and genetic engineering. For this reason little remained from the first draft other than the concept.

As with the first draft, the angle I took was to write as one of the offenders, as in:

... since *we* first set foot on her surface
IN THE PAST 100 YEARS *OUR* ASSAULTS HAVE GROWN WORSE

But as the piece progressed I found this more personal style less effective in that I was admitting responsibility and writing from a reader's point of view. Nevertheless, some of the vocabulary used was aggressive and hard-hitting, but the introduction of speech marks around some phrases made the piece too personal by making the language informal, so lessening its effect, for example, 'messed up big', 'So what?'.

The attack on 'the generation in power ...' was prompted by bigoted attitudes encountered when members of this generation read the first draft, dismissing it with a blasé, 'It won't be my problem in a few years' attitude.

I found the use of examples helpful in strengthening the impact. For example, the description of the Romans' abuse perhaps has a certain shock value in that it reminds the reader that mankind has '... abused and raped planet Earth since we first set foot on her surface.'

When, towards the end of the piece, I needed to give it a message, that is, persuade the audience to do something, I felt the result was rather vague. It seemed to be a cross between 'Keep Britain Tidy' and join a 'Green' party, hence any emotion that had been built up by the passage was frustrated in its attempt to find expression. Alternatively the ending could be seen as a message telling teenagers it is up to them to correct the world's problems.

Third draft

Due to a realisation that to persuade teenagers to be conscious of the environment was less challenging and perhaps less productive than trying to change the minds of a middle-aged audience, I decided to present this draft as a leaflet to be distributed by a 'Green' party as an aid to the recruitment of middle-aged members.

I found the pun on the phrase 'What on earth are you doing?' effective in that this is usually a trivial rebuke, and to apply it to such a major subject is unusual and hence it is foregrounded. I have since seen a Channel 4 programme called 'What on earth is going on?' which deals with environmental issues. However I arrived at my title before I saw this programme.

As the audience, I believe, would be somewhat difficult to persuade to read a piece of writing severely criticising them in its entirety, I employed all the graphical means at my disposal to encourage them to read on. The final sentence is typed in upper case letters to provide a mental bridge, easing the reader from the title into the text. Similarly, various important statements are printed in upper case letters both to highlight them and to make the text more appealing/interesting to the eye. The two questions which are the focus of the whole piece are printed in extra large type to attract attention.

The register of the draft has altered. I wrote it not as one of the offenders but as an observer, perhaps, as is suggested by, 'Your generation really does not care', a member of the teenage generation. I made the language as bitter and aggressive as I could, consciously searching through the second draft and changing any words I considered too mild, hence:

'removing'	became	'stripped'
'blanket'	became	'shroud'
'released'	became	'contaminated'

As I was attacking a generation whose blasé attitude seemed to be that they would be dead before it becomes really bad, I decided to remind them of their descendants and more especially their children having to live with the legacy. I believe that this may possibly stir some emotion or at least provoke thought amongst the intended audience, which in turn may persuade them to take action and so the leaflet will have succeeded. Therefore the devastation of the reader's offspring is stressed several times:

'Imagine your children having to suffer'
'... you are condemning your offspring ...'

I did not have to avoid any 'difficult' vocabulary as I would have had to were I writing for a young audience, so terms such as 'pogrom' and 'voracious pillage' were added to strengthen the aggressive, disaster oriented vocabulary without fear that they would be either misunderstood or not comprehended at all.

Grammatical changes were made so as to create a more correct piece which could less easily be scoffed at or dismissed by sceptics as a poorly produced piece. Hence:

'mixed with rainw-ater' – hyphenated words were correctly separated
'on land, sea and air' became 'in the sea and air and on the land'

The final draft had a much more definite message, that is – join a Green party – and hence the argument was more effective. Once again playing upon the audience's fear for their children, I was able to link up the title with the penultimate question and then leave the reader to ponder the final, perhaps prophetic, question about how future generations would view the present generation's tenure of the planet.

Conclusion

The success of this piece as a means of recruiting people to a 'Green' party cannot be judged, as the party is fictional, and the leaflet has not reached a wide circulation. So, to attempt to gain some comment on its validity I sent a copy to Greenpeace, inviting them to remark on its strengths and weaknesses. As yet I have had no reply.

On showing the leaflet to various middle-aged people they have informed me that it raised various emotions, from anger at being blamed and accused to sadness at the fact that they feel so helpless. This shows that by the third draft the piece had achieved one of its primary objectives, to stir emotion. This is an improvement upon the first draft which was quickly dismissed by several readers.

Therefore I can say that through careful development and redrafting, the piece has achieved a certain amount of success and perhaps persuaded a few people to respect their environment a little more.

Appraisal of a commentary such as this is subject to similar caveats which cover any piece of criticism; for example the paradox that an author may not fully understand, indeed may *misunderstand*, her or his own text. As users of language we have only limited access through introspection to the processes which result in utterances and acts of understanding. We mistake *post hoc* desires to fulfil the expectations of teachers, syllabuses and long-held presuppositions for intentions. We try to avoid presenting ourselves as authors in too bad a light, for example by understating the influence of sources. But given these difficulties, this student's commentary seems quite successful. It has the advantage of referring to a powerful and clearly structured text whose topic is generally acknowledged to be important, it develops in complexity of response, depth of insight and confidence as it proceeds, and it has something to say about all the important constituents of a text – author's point of view, relation to audience, purposes, tone, structure, lexis.

Comments on the first draft are mainly concerned with lexical and structural matters, though the problem of audience, which determines much of the direction in which the commentary unfolds, is mentioned.

The commentary on the second draft describes a sensible narrowing down of content, from all the world's problems to just the major environmental ones, a simultaneous shift in authorial point of view and intended audience, and a conscious reduction in the informality of the text. It also describes the problem of how the text might focus, rather than dissipate, the emotion it has generated.

In her commentary on the third draft, this student has refined the purpose of her text and specified her intended audience quite precisely. By this means she has allowed herself scope for more aggressive lexis than would have been appropriate for a text with a subtler or more cajoling tone. The examples she gives of considered substitutions are rather unconvincing. It is doubtful whether simple replacement of lexical items along a single dimension often forms part of the redrafter's repertoire. But the examples, and her following observations about using 'difficult' vocabulary, point to the sense of freedom to use vocabulary outside her everyday range given to this author by her choice of *tone* (formal), *point of view* (committed but detached observer) and *audience* (middle-aged people).

She also makes two important defensive moves. She ensures that matters of hyphenation and preposition usage conform to convention, perhaps having become aware through contact with her 'bigoted' first draft readers that deviation from 'correctness' makes a text of this kind vulnerable to irrelevant but damaging criticism. She has also refined such surface features as print type to help overcome what she recognizes will be her readers' resistance to the text's accusing tone.

She discusses both the title and the ending, and though the forms used to resolve problems associated with parts of the text are in many ways very similar, she does not link them. She concludes with a modest claim for the text's success as measured by reader response.

7 Investigating language

Much of the discussion about what teachers need to know about language has focused on the content of their degree, pre-service and inservice education courses. What is the most appropriate ratio of literature to language study at first degree level? How much Linguistics should there be in PGCE, BEd and other English courses to ensure that future English teachers can cope with the Knowledge About Language component of the National Curriculum? The longing for a body of knowledge in English is strong, but many teachers have sensibly resisted it; the evidence from the development of A Level English Language is that classroom teachers and lecturers can and do develop rigorous and practical frameworks for language study, drawing on a wide variety of sources, including the language environment, their observation of pupils' and students' talk and writing, literature, as well as areas of academic linguistics.

The need for teachers and their pupils and students to have well-principled theoretical frameworks and discovery methods is nowhere more urgently felt than in the area of non-standard usage of language. Many of the most deeply ingrained prejudices can be traced back to very basic conceptual confusions, many of them perpetuated for motives of social status, political control and economic power. Indeed the prejudices are often most firmly believed by non-standard users themselves, so all-pervading is the message that non-standard equals substandard. The liberal response, to appeal for tolerance and equality of esteem as abstract principles, may help to create a more positive mind-set towards language, but it is quite possible to subscribe to the slogans in principle while at the same time treating standard forms as yardsticks because the theoretical frameworks and background of investigation are not sufficiently well established to offer alternative perspectives. For example, the following commentary on a short text of written Jamaican English is representative of the strategies students use to discuss non-standard forms. It was written as an answer to a question on the *Language varieties* section of the 1991 JMB A Level English Language Paper 1 which offered a Jamaican English (JE) text alongside a Standard British English (SBE) version. It may be that the presence of the SBE version pre-empted the student's response, implicitly suggesting its use as a point of departure. The student may have responded to aspects of the orthography used in writing the Jamaican English, such as apostrophes and non-standard spelling. Or he may not have been sufficiently familiar with Jamaican English to be able to treat it as a self-sufficient language system, and therefore overassimilated it to the variety of English with which he was most familiar. Whatever the reason, this analysis suggests an urgent need for students to have access to sensible, accurate and objective ways of talking about language. The question is given here, and the student's answer follows immediately.

JMB A Level English Language Paper 1 1991 Question 3(b)

Language varieties

Lennox Alexander, a fifth form boy at Hackney Downs School, London, wrote two versions of the same event, one in Standard English and one in Jamaican English. He chose to write about an occasion when rival groups played select-ed discs in a Hifi challenge contest. The first two paragraphs of each version are printed below.

Describe some of the linguistic features of Jamaican English in *Version 2* below, and comment on the range of attitudes held towards this variety. If you wish, you may refer to *Version 1*, and to other sources as appropriate.

Version 1　Mafia Versus King Tubby
This is set at a Friday club in Stoke Newington where the battle of the sound systems was taking place. The ever popular Mafia hifi was taking on King Tubby's Hifi. Tony Jones was the dub controller for Mafia Hifi and Cedric Shaw for King Tubby. There was about a couple of hundred people there and forty speakers, twenty-five of which belonged to Mafia.

At last they started to warm up, testing mikes and making sure all speakers were connected properly and working. Meanwhile some of the older boys rolled up their splifs[1] and the younger ones begged, mostly in vain, for a draw. The atmosphere was very tense with the crowd arguing bitterly as to who would win.

Version 2　Mafia Versus King Tubby
Dis 'ere did set down a Friday Club, Stoke Newington where dem was 'aving a bakkle of soun' wid Mafia tekking on King Tubby Hifi. Tony Jones was dub controller fe Mafia an' Cedric Shaw fe Tubby an' dem. Dere was seh about forty box in de 'all, an' about twenty five of dem belong to Mafia. Before de soun' dem ready, de place was awready jam out wid seh 'bout couple 'undred rudies.

Dem soon start to warm up, tes'ing mikes and mekking sure dat all speaker an' ting was connect up an' working good. Meanwhile some o' de older de rudy was buil'ing up dem splif' an' de smaller bwoy child dem try to capture off even if i's only a likkle draw. Everybody full up wid excitement and plenty people was arguing wid each aneddur 'bout who would win.

(from The Talk Workshop Group, 1982)

¹splif – a cigarette containing marijuana   .

Candidate's answer to JMB A Level English Language Question 3(b) Paper 1 1991: Mafia Versus King Tubby

Version 2 of the extract is written in Jamaican English. The most obvious feature of this extract is the way it is phonetically spelt to represent the sounds and pronunciation of the words.

A feature of Jamaican English which is shown in the extract is where the phonetic symbol (δ) in 'the' is replaced by the letter 'd' to give 'dem' instead of 'them' and also (θ) is replaced by 'd'.

Ellipses of letters occur quite frequently, for example ' 'aving' (having), 'tes'ing' (testing) ' 'bout' (about). This gives us a clearer idea of how Jamaican English is spoken.

At the beginning of *Version 2* it opens with 'Dis 'ere did set down a Friday Club'. Compared with *Version 1* you can see that the word ' 'ere' is used to represent 'here' and there is the addition of 'did' which may be used as 'is' in Standard English. There is also 'down' to mean 'at', so in Standard English it is 'This is set at a Friday Club', whereas in Jamaican English they use different words with the addition of words to the passage, compared to the Standard English version.

Jamaican English does not show the different tenses whether present, future or past and if so the tense is usually different when compared with Standard English e.g. 'did set down a Friday Club'. Standard English e.g. 'is set at a Friday Club'. In Jamaican English the words 'did set down' means to me that it is in the past tense in that it 'was set at a Friday Club'.

You also get 'dem was' instead of 'they were', again to do with tenses.

One of the biggest ellipses of letters is the letter 'd' usually at the end of words, e.g. 'soun' ', 'an' '.

I did notice that the Jamaican English used the word 'rudies' to mean 'people', which is probably part of their slang.

Also, throughout *Version 2*, words which contained a double 'tt' were replaced by a double 'kk' e.g. 'likkle', 'bakkle' etc.

There is also an ellipsis of the ending 'ed' e.g. in Standard English you have 'started', in Jamaican English they use 'start' so that it is in the wrong tense.

Jamaican English users don't tend to use plurals e.g. 'speaker' instead of 'speakers'. .   .

The Standard English version tends to use more elaborate words e.g. 'vain', 'systems' and 'atmosphere', whereas the Jamaican English version tends to use simplified words e.g. 'speaker', 'an' ting' and 'jam' (crowded). In *Version 1* they use 'argue bitterly' whereas *Version 2* uses 'arguing wid each aneddur' (another) which is a lot more simplified.

They also use 'o' ' to represent 'of', but sometimes in Jamaican English you can get the merging of (δ) and (θ) to (f) and (v) e.g. 'bruvver' and 'ruf' or 'def' (death).

Attitudes towards Jamaican English vary depending on social economic classes, for example a refined RP speaker would compare it as being lazy, slang, the dialect/accent of a lower socio-economic class, e.g. working class, due to its sloppy pronunciation, and maybe even as incorrect.

Whereas children and younger generations, e.g. students, may see it as being fashionable and 'trendy' and by using the language may be a form of badge membership to a group excluding people who are unable to use the language. What we must consider before criticising a language is 'dialects are no better nor worse, nor poorer or corrupt. Just different' (Edwina Newman).

There is no such thing as incorrect, it is a matter of appropriateness!

The answer's main strategy for comment is to describe features of Jamaican English in terms of their difference from Standard British English using a variety of forms of words to express these differences:

the phonetic symbol (δ) in '*the*' is replaced by the letter 'd'
Ellipses of letters occur quite frequently
there is the addition of 'did'
in Jamaican English they use different words with the addition of words
You also get 'dem was' instead of 'they were'
... ellipses of letters is the letter 'd' usually at the end of words
words which contained a double 'tt' were replaced by a double 'kk'
... ellipsis of the ending 'ed'
'start' ... is in the wrong tense
Jamaican English users don't tend to use plurals
the Jamaican English version tends to use simplified words
in Jamaican English you can get the merging of (δ) and (θ) to (f) and (v)

To some extent the vocabulary of *ellipsis, replacement, addition, simplification* is encouraged by some aspects of the text itself. For example, the JE writer has used an orthography which marks aspects of his language use which he perceives as significant, even where a fluent speaker of SBE could not accurately be described as missing sounds out; for example, 'ere, 'aving, an'. It is also true that many studies of Jamaican English have tended to focus on differences between SBE and JE, and knowledge of these may have influenced this analysis. However, a descriptive commentary might have noted a range of ways of expressing plurality, including:

- *Words which seem to be intrinsically plural*
  'dem' used as a pronoun, e.g. 'Dem soon start to warm up ...'
- *Words marked as plural by suffixes*
  'dem', e.g. 'de soun' dem' *or* 'de smaller bwoy child dem'
  -s, e.g. 'couple' undred rudies' *or* 'tes'ing mikes'
- *Words marked as plural by determiners and/or premodifiers*
  (i)   number + noun, e.g. 'forty box'
  (ii) quantity premodifier or determiner + noun or noun phrase, e.g. 'all speaker' *or* 'some o' de older de rudy' *or* 'dem splif'

Together with a more detailed knowledge of varieties of JE, these data might tend to suggest that Lennox Alexander has chosen to use a form of JE which is comprehensible to speakers of SBE. If a JE speaker chooses, out of consideration for his readers and his sense of the formality of written forms, to do this, it hardly seems appropriate to criticize his use of language for falling short of SBE.

Describing linguistic features of JE represents a considerable challenge for students who have only a sketchy and deficiency-centred idea of how language works. As we saw in Chapter 1, part of the answer is a greater determination to take students' own language experience seriously, whether that experience is rooted in SBE, a regional dialect, ethnic variety or other language. Descriptive frameworks of the kind illustrated by the categorization of plural in JE also have an important part to play in allowing pupils and students to discover for themselves that language varieties have their own distinctive ways of realizing concepts which we may take for granted in our own uses of language. And pupils and students need, above all, to test their ideas and discovery procedures against empirical data which they have derived for themselves if positive attitudes are not to become mere counter-prejudices.

Gains made through well-principled investigation may be partial and painstakingly achieved against the tide of conventional thinking, but the fact that they can be made at all offers some grounds for optimism. One example relates to another examination by an A Level English Language student of English used by speakers who have access to West Indian-related varieties of English. In this case, the investigation was carried out as an A Level English Language *Investigation into Language Use*, or *Project*.

An analysis of Black English

In its 'Introduction', this Project gives a brief history of the development of West Indian Creoles, focusing particularly on West Indian English in the UK, with an account of relations between the UK and the West Indies, including patterns of immigration into the UK. The writer comments that:

> Unfortunately, no linguistic studies were made of the Creole during their actual evolution. This is mainly because of what David Sutcliffe describes as 'eighteenth century prejudices against non-standard dialect and "uncivilised" society'.

The Project analyses the language of two speakers, one of whom came to work in Britain at the age of seventeen, the other being born in Britain. The stated aims of the study are:

> To examine the differences and similarities between the languages used by each speaker, to compare observed Creole forms with SE and to draw conclusions about the language change which is currently taking place in British Black English.

Two speakers were interviewed in informal surroundings, the interviews transcribed and the transcripts used as a basis for comment on and analysis of lexical and grammatical features. The writer commented that

> this method ... was not as successful as had been hoped. The Creole features in the language of both speakers became considerably less as soon as the interview began.

Some extracts from the transcripts are as follows (dots in brackets indicate brief pauses; numbers in brackets indicate the lengths of longer pauses in seconds):

Interview with Ricky

[Ricky came to Britain from St Kitts at the age of 17.]

Interviewer: how old were you when you first came to England? (1.0)
Ricky: seventeen
Interviewer: and (.) before that (.) what did you used to do in St Kitts? (1.0)
Ricky: wha'y mean wha' I don' used to do? (1.0)
Interviewer: em (.) were you at school there or did you work?
Ricky: I was working (.) stop from school when I was fourteen
Interviewer: what was school like there? (3.0)
Ricky: wha' was it like? wha' y'mean wha' was it like? like a school (.) dey go school to learn (.) innit? (1.0) yeah well? I went an' I learn (1.0)
Interviewer: was the teacher really strict? (2.0)
Ricky: uh yeah (.) in a way you can say da' (3.0) cos if you din learn (1.0) you get lick 'nstead

Interview with Jean

[Jean was born and educated in the UK. Her parents are from Jamaica, and have always spoken to Jean in Creole. The topic in this part of the transcript is a recent visit by Jean to the USA.]

Interviewer: and er what's the lifestyle like over there is it very different to here?
Jean: yeah it's very different (.) it's (.) em (.) people (.) out there work (.) extremely hard (.) em (.) there's
Interviewer: mm
Jean: (.) em many people work twenty-four hours a day (.) work (.) all night and (.) even the day (.)
Interviewer: mm
Jean: a lot of people 'ave two jobs as well (.) as
Interviewer: mm
Jean: well as [laughs] 'avin' two cars (1.0) yeah but em the lifestyle's very different I mean it was really hot an' (.) sunny out there and (.) people jus' dressed casually all the time in shorts and (1.0) swimsuits

A detailed commentary on Ricky's and Jean's pronunciation followed, including such observations as:

1 In Standard English/RP the meanings of 'want' and 'one' /wont/ and /won/ are clear as the final consonant 't' marks the distinction. In Creole, however, 't' as a final consonant is rarely pronounced, but the meanings of 'one' and 'want' are still clear because the vowel sound changes: /wæn/ (one) /won/ (want)

2 (At one point in the interview) Ricky gives the reply,
'no no really...'

The first 'no' is pronounced /nɔ/ and the second /no/, indicating a difference in meaning: 'no, not really'.

3 Ricky often uses the usual SE pronunciation of /ð/, e.g.
'my mother'
'... I was there'

4 He also uses the Creole pronunciation, /d/, e.g.
'... me moder is goin' 'ome'
'... you stayed dere wid me.'

5 The /d/ is used much more frequently than the /ð/ in his speech. Jean also uses both /ð/ and /d/, e.g.
'*th*e polytechnic ...'
'... I'm not sure about *th*at'
'... eight broders ...'
'... lumbered down wi' de work'

However, she uses the SE /ð/ much more frequently than the Creole /d/.

The transcripts provided a rich source of commentary on syntax, including the following:

- Sutcliffe points out that broad Creole has an optional plural marker; the particle '-dem'. Ricky shows one example of its usage: '... dere's people back 'ome ... who speak better ... English dan some o' de white man-dem.'
- Earlier in the transcript there is an example of hypercorrection of plural forms. Ricky applies the SE rule of adding '-s' to form a plural to the uncountable noun 'work':
'... we 'ave different kin' a *works* jus' like 'ere.'

Jean uses a plural form where it is incorrect in SE:
'... I do a bit of sports now an' again ...'

This is possibly another example of hypercorrection.

- Ricky shows a strong tendency to express past tense meaning using present tense forms, e.g.

  '... I went an' I learn ...'
  '... I stop from school when I was fourteen ...'
  '... like the question wha' you ask ...'

- Jean uses a greater variety of tenses than Ricky. She constructs most of her verbs in the usual SE way, e.g.

  '... that involves cooking dishes'
  'people just dressed casually ...'

The Project found little evidence of distinctive differences in lexis between SE and Creole. Only one convincing example was recorded:

  '... dey cut der jibberidge' [they use their language]

The Project's evaluation and conclusion comments on several points of interest, including:

Evidence for the existence of a Creole continuum, affecting pronunciation and grammar in particular
The tendency of younger speakers to approximate more closely to RP and SE than older speakers
The importance of language as a part of people's 'ethnic identity'
The difficulties of finding an appropriate written representation of West Indian Creole
The likelihood or otherwise that West Indian Creole will survive as a distinct linguistic form in the UK

This investigation into language use represents a significant advance on the examination answer. It offers a historical and a social context, and a recognition of the need for an informal situation as a background to informant interviews. Having faced up to some of the methodological problems of collecting data, and the practical problems of transferring speech into writing without access to an authorized orthography, the student is able to work from a body of data in which she has invested considerable time and effort. Interpreting her data presses home the need for a wide-ranging and detailed theoretical framework as a prerequisite for meaningful description.

But even with these advantages, the writer is unable fully to break free from the same Standard English-centred assumptions which betrayed the examination candidate into linguistic confusion. Much of the Project's commentary on pronunciation is dominated by the use of an idealized form of RP as a paradigm. For example:

- Both speakers always omit the consonant /h/ and often replace it with a glottal stop /ʔ/, e.g.

  '... when I go' ʔere firs'

- Although many final consonants are dropped in Ricky's speech when they are part of a consonant cluster, /t/ is dropped when it is not part of a cluster, e.g.

  'wha'' [*what*]
  'abou' da'' [*about that*]

- Where consonant clusters occur at the end of a word, Ricky drops the final consonant in almost every case, e.g.

  'don''   (t)
  'jus''   (t)
  'in fac'' (t)
  'an''   (d)
  'drin''   (k)

- Ricky also occasionally drops a consonant from a cluster appearing in the middle of a word, e.g.

  'y' un'erstan'' [you understand]

- Jean rarely drops other consonants from a cluster. Rare occurrences of this include:

  'sal' fish' (t)
  'an''   (d)
  'jus''   (t)

The term 'sal' fish' is one which Jean will probably be used to hearing pronounced by West Indians rather than by Standard English speakers.

A substantial part of the commentary on syntax adopts the same stance. For example:

- Ricky usually forms his plurals in the correct SE way, e.g.

  'guys'
  'white men'
  'pubs'
  'matches'

- Jean omits the definite article, e.g.

  'I'm studying about hotel and catering industry ...'

- She also frequently omits the indefinite article, e.g.

  'had absolutely great time ...'
  'it's Pentacostal Church ...'
  'it's Jamaican fruit ...'

- Ricky omits the inflected ending from the third person singular of the present tense:

  '... so I might jus' wait till she go home.'

However, it is clear that the writer of this Project would have much less difficulty than the examination candidate in working away from the Standard English-centred perspective which so limits potential for wider language awareness.

The key issue is not how much Linguistics there should be on the English curriculum, but the empirical question of how speakers and writers draw on the systems of language, grammatical, semantic, pragmatic, in order to create and negotiate meanings, and how they can be encouraged to develop and extend the relevant processes. The issue can be stated in a variety of different terms: *de Saussurean* – what is the relation between *la langue* (the abstract system of language) and *la parole* (actual utterances)?; *Chomskian* – how does language *performance* emerge from language *competence*?; *Hallidean* – how is *meaning potential* realized?

If teachers of English are to intervene successfully in their pupils' and students' language development, they need adequate practical and theoretical frameworks to understand how learners deploy elements of the language system they have internalized. For example, there is enough data in the following short extract from a Year 8 pupil's spontaneous experiment with noun phrase- and word-formation to investigate some important concepts in English morphology and syntax:

The time machine

[The narrator wishes to build an improved version of his time machine.]

I got home and ripped out all the old pieces of the Mark I machine, and delved into my collection of wonderful devices to see what I should put in it and I found: a new hydraulic converter, a transdimensional technocosmic molecule separator, a constant velocity reciprocator, a supercharging woffle-agitating tube, a retrosearch translocation matrix, a triple density solenoidal activator, an alphawave decompressor and a roll of soft and gentle pink toilet paper.

The problem of how to define the term 'word' is raised by such compounds as 'woffleagitating' and 'alphawave'; do these terms count as one single word, or as two? The idea that lexical items in English do not necessarily coincide with words is illustrated in the words 'transdimensional' and 'translocation'. The meaning of both items is quite clear: the first means across spatial and/or temporal dimensions, the second means across spatial, and possibly temporal, positions, and both would clearly be necessary for an effective time machine. But the lexical status of 'trans-' is different from that of 'dimensional' and 'location', since these terms can be used independently whereas 'trans-' cannot. A survey of the extract reveals other words which consist of separable units of meaning, some of which can be used independently (free items) and some of which can not (bound items):

Bound items	Free items
trans	dimensional
techno	cosmic
retro	search
de	compressor

A closer examination reveals that bound items also occur after free items. For example;

Free items	Bound items
dimension	al
separat(e)	or
reciprocat(e)	or
- charg(e)	ing
-agitat(e)	ing
-locat(e)	ion
dens(e)	ity
solenoid	al
activ(e)	at(e) or
(de)compress	or

The passage is also a useful source of data for examining the structure of noun phrases. The 'scientific' phrases tend to be premodified:

Premodifier(s)	Head
a new hydraulic	converter
a transdimensional technocosmic molecule	separator
a constant velocity	reciprocator
a supercharging woffleagitating	tube
a retrosearch translocation	matrix
a triple density solenoidal	activator
an alphawave	decompressor

However, others are postmodified:

Premodifiers	Head	Postmodifiers
all the old	pieces	of the Mark I machine
my	collection	of wonderful devices
a	roll	of soft and gentle pink toilet paper

And the postmodifiers themselves contain premodifiers and a head:

Premodifier(s)	Head
the Mark I	machine
wonderful	devices
soft and gentle pink toilet	paper

This writer is drawing on such morphological and syntactic resources to create a parody of the scientific register, and thereby to achieve an imaginative effect. But the parody only works because it has some semantic verisimilitude 'Retrosearch translocation matrix', for example, is not an arbitrary phrase in the context of time travel. And the description contains some clues about how a time machine might work with its 'transdimensional techno-cosmic molecule separator'. I can't help thinking that the writer might be using a 'woffleagitating tube' as a device for creating the passage's over-charged style. Any teacher would share this pupil's delight in playing with language, but a teacher who could also recognize that he is experimenting with morphology, syntax and meanings simultaneously, using highly marked and register-specific structures within the secure confines of humour, can begin to see possibilities for development. What other registers might be parodied in this way? – fashion journalism? travel writing? What other ways might there be of encouraging pupils to explore complex words and phrases? How else can we encourage pupils to build imaginative constructs that extend their sense of the power of language?

Teachers must find practical responses to challenges such as these if learners' general understanding of language is to become rooted in their own language experience, and if opportunities for feedback and continuity are not to be lost. This book has tried to suggest some ways of creating conditions which favour fruitful interaction between different aspects and levels of language. We saw in Chapter 3, 'Speaking and Writing', that speech and writing can feed back into each other. Chapter 6, 'Relating Language Study and Language Experience at 16+', discussed some of the ways in which pupils and students can use their understanding of language to enrich the way they write. This chapter, 'Investigating Language', has been concerned with using empirical study of language to help learners deepen their sense of what it means to be a language user. But these possibilities for feedback can only be realized if we are prepared to create forums in which learners can discuss, debate and explore the language issues that matter to them. In this respect, familiar methods such as discussion, narrative writing and active reading have their part to play in creating curriculum space for exploring these issues at 16+ as well as with younger children.

A sense of the potential for continuity can be illustrated by two different explorations of aspects of language acquisition. The first, *Baby Talk*, was written by a Year 8 pupil in response to a discussion of what it might be like to perceive the world from a baby's point of view. The second, *Learning Labels*, consists of extracts from an examination essay written by a 16+ A Level English Language student.

Baby talk

(Courtesy of Karen Dunn, Brookvale County High School, Warrington)

'I've said it once and I'll say it again. Stevie looks just like his father did when he was a boy.'

'Except his eyes, he's got his mother's eyes ...'

Just shut up. I look like myself. I can't stand it when people compare me with other people. Especially my Grandad and Grandma. They just stand there and gape at me as if I'm an alien. Then they start making pathetic noises.

Oh no. It's that big man that calls himself daddy. Aaaarrrhh it's a raspberry, and on my stomach. What a cheek. HA, HA, Ha, Ha, OH NO, STOP, Please STOP. It was a tickle. I wouldn't mind but my dad's hands are so big, and they know exactly where to tickle me and make me laugh.

What's that?

'Dinny dins. Come on it's a choo choo train. Open wide, into the tunnel. Choo, choo.'

Oh, mum. Errgg. Cow Gate roast beef. From now on I'm a vegetarian. So don't give me any more. I said don't give me any more. They've stopped trying to feed me, thank God. God, who is God? Oh well, nothing to worry about yet.

I'm going to sleep now as I've got to catch up on my beauty sleep. Good night.

Learning labels

Children develop an understanding of the meanings and usage of English words by basically acquiring a word then putting it into practice. They work out the *specific* object it labels but often use it for other objects where they see similarities until they have acquired other words to name these objects .... So the brain of a child in acquiring language is going through a trial-and-error process, slotting in and swapping around information to enable himself to develop an understanding of words' meanings and usage .... Children will not accept words that label everything. They like to be specific in what they label. A child is able to see the difference between a cow and a dog. This was shown in an experiment where a child called various objects that were either round, shiny or green 'apple', but when presented with a tray containing some of the objects labelled 'apple' as well as an apple, she could pick out straight away the real apple.

The writer of *Baby Talk* is offered narrative conventions which allow her to sidestep the philosophical problems of how to describe the underlying rules of young children's utterances on their own terms when access to the relevant point of view is only possible through language which is by definition more conceptually sophisticated than the language it is attempting to describe. Some interesting issues are raised; for example: How far do baby-talk, such as 'Dinny dins', and ritual actions, such as the train metaphor which accompanies feeding, facilitate language learning? What is the role of physical contact, such as tickling, in laying a foundation of symbolic interaction? What are the origins of the affective functions of language, for example 'pathetic', 'What a cheek'? Is a sense of self – 'I look like myself' – possible without language? But most of the focus is on the behaviour of adults, with only an occasional hint of how a baby might attempt to code objects and sensations with limited conceptual resources. The account's concern is much more to create an ironic sense of the strangeness of ordinary actions and familiar concepts. How, for example, do we come to understand such complex ideas as brand names, vegetarianism and God? Each requires, in its own way, familiarity with some of the social, economic, evaluative and cultural institutions into which the infant is about to begin the process of being socialized.

As might be expected, the 16+ student's account is more abstract, more formal and more directly focused on linguistic matters. It refers, in general terms, to *operations* and *relations between processes* (for example, 'acquiring a word then putting it into practice'), *criteria* (for example, 'where they see similarities'), *hypotheses* (for example, 'a trial-and-error process'), *heuristics* (for example, the use of words as temporary labels) and *paradigms* (for example, in the reference to the experiment which showed that children can recognize central cases even when they overgeneralize).

These two accounts may seem to offer reference points for continuity: the younger pupil uses first-person imaginative internal monologue to create a particular situation. The older student employs the third person and achieves a more objective stance to consider general principles of acquisition. On this model, the possibility for continuity consists in the presence of common underlying concerns; the view of children using language to develop control of their social and physical environments, and the implied conception in both accounts of children as active participants in their own language development. But this view may be specious. A discussion of principles might have allowed the Year 8 pupil to enter more fully and imaginatively into a prelinguistic perspective, and the challenge of adopting a narrative point of view might have helped the 16+ student to explore in more specific terms what may be involved in such vaguely defined processes as seeing similarities and 'slotting in and swapping round information'. Such reversals might also help pupils and students to see how an understanding of language acquisition can enrich their own language development. *Baby Talk* brings out quite clearly the complexity and interdependence of concepts mastered by its author, while acknowledging how far there is yet to go. The willingness to experiment and the desire for accuracy of description commented on in *Learning Labels* might also benefit the way its author uses language.

As in every other field of language, contributions to development work both ways. Strong interests resist open dialogue about anything but the narrowest and most functional concerns of language, but continuity across the 11–16/16+ divide requires a determination by teachers to keep open the channels between those aspects of language which pupils and students can themselves use to move their own language development forward, accreting vocabulary and technical skills, but also widening their sense of what it is to participate in a language, a community and a culture by continually reshaping their language experience.

References

Burke, J. (1978). *Life in the Castle in Medieval England*. London, Batsford.

'Call for a ban on 'war' toys' (1983). In *New World*.

Carter, D. (1988). 'Quaint Moonmarks', in M. Jones, and A. West, *Learning Me Your Language*. London, Mary Glasgow.

DES (1990). *English for Ages 5 to 16*. London, HMSO.

Doughty, P., Pearce, J. and Thornton, G. (1971). *Language in Use*. London, Edward Arnold.

Fletcher, P. (1985). *A Child's Learning of English*. Oxford, Blackwell.

Freestone, B. (1968). *The Pegasus Book of Good English*. London, Dennis Dobson.

Greenwell B. (1988). *Alternatives at English A Level*. Sheffield, NATE.

Keen, J. (1978). *Teaching English: A Linguistic Approach*. London, Methuen.

Keen, J. (1989). *The Language Awareness Project Years 7–9; Language for Talking, Living and Learning*. Lancaster, Framework Press.

Knight, R. (1987). 'English as it is written – and as it should be taught', *The Guardian*, 2 June.

Mackay, D., Thompson, B. and Schaub, P. (1970). *Breakthrough to Literacy*. Schools Council Programme in Linguistics and English Teaching. London, Longman.

Marvell, A. (1967). 'The Coronet', in H. Gardner (ed.), *The Metaphysical Poets*. Oxford, Oxford University Press.

Mittins, W. H. (1991). *Language Awareness for Teachers*. Milton Keynes, Open University Press.

'Revised Phantom' (1986). In *Aircraft Illustrated*.

The Talk Workshop Group (1982). *Becoming Our Own Experts*. Distributed by ILEA English Centre, London.

Whiteley, M. (1988). 'English Language at A Level', in *English A Level in Practice*, NATE Post 14 Committee. Sheffield, NATE.

Wright, P. (1974). *The Language of British Industry*. Basingstoke, Macmillan.

Index

Note: Mention is made so often in the text to such terms as language study, talking, dialect, Standard English, National Curriculum that it is impossible to include them in the index.